# —THE—
# INNER STORM

# —THE— INNER STORM

ALMA J. YATES

Deseret Book Company
Salt Lake City, Utah

First printing October 1988

**Library of Congress Cataloging-in-Publication Data**

Yates, Alma J.
    The inner storm
        p.   cm.
    ISBN 0-87579-175-1 : $9.95 (est.)
    I. Title.
PS3575.A755I5   1988
813'.54 — dc19                                   88-23486
                                                    CIP

*To Ralph Brown*

# Chapter One

I hadn't expected Mom in Colonia Juarez until dark, or even the next day, just before Grandpa's funeral. Of course, in the back of my mind I knew she was coming. After all, Grandpa was her own father. And yet, I hadn't really thought of her coming. Ever since learning of Grandpa's death my mind had been a turmoil of shock and disbelief. Perhaps it is impossible to understand and accept death in a matter of hours, especially when there's been no opportunity for preparation or forethought. It takes time to sift through the hurt, the confusion, and the loss. I was still engulfed in that painful sifting process when I came around the corner of Grandpa's barn after helping Reese Taylor put away a load of hay. I was pulling off my leather gloves and slapping hay leaves from my pants and shirt when I saw Mom step from our maroon Buick. It was like seeing an acquaintance step from a far-distant past.

I stopped, totally surprised. Her shock was no less than mine. She looked tired, worn out — even older. Maybe that was from the trip or the news of Grandpa's death. His death had taken us all by surprise. Mom caught her breath momentarily. Then she smiled, a forced smile, taut with uncertainty. And almost as soon as the smile appeared, it flickered and faded into a mask of cautious solemnity. Nervously she gnawed at her lower lip, all the while holding the car keys in a clenched, white-knuckled fist. She had had her keys the last time. I

1

remembered that. I remembered most everything about that last time. I would have preferred to forget, but memories like that, tainted with guilt, tend to linger and nag.

For a moment neither of us spoke, but instinctively I knew it was my move. Weeks earlier, when we had fumbled through our clumsy farewell, she had been the last to speak. I wet my lips and nodded my head once. "Hi, Mom." I smiled. "It's good . . . " I swallowed. "It's good to see you." I took a step toward her, leaned down, and kissed her on the cheek.

Tears welled up in her eyes. She put her arms around my neck and pulled me close. For a long moment she held me there, grasped tightly in her embrace. I didn't pull away as I had done at times when I was at home. Instead, I allowed her those few moments just to hold me. I guessed that the emotion and the embrace was for both Grandpa and me.

Finally she pushed herself back. Wiping tears from her eyes, she looked me up and down, swallowed back her emotion, and asked, "Have you grown or—" She pressed her lips together. "Or do you just look different?"

I laughed. "I've probably grown. Lots. Grandma wouldn't ever let me go hungry." I felt my cheeks color. "A guy grows a lot in the summer."

"You do *look* different."

I nodded, smiling. I *was* different, so very different from the guy who had walked into the border immigration office at Palomas, Mexico. I remembered it all so clearly. And yet, it was as though I was looking back on a stranger now.

The office was small, stuffy and stale with sweat and foul tobacco smoke. The white walls, spotted and smudged with grime and dirty fingerprints, were uninviting and bare with the exception of a dog-eared, out-of-date calendar and a huge portrait of de la Madrid, president of Mexico. Three metal office desks cramped the small oblong room, and a motley assortment of scarred and battered chairs crowded the wall in front of the main desk. Several flies buzzed and pinged incessantly at the windows, and the dull drone of an electric fan struggled to breathe coolness into the heavy air.

The immigration officer, a swarthy man with a trimmed mustache, lazily studied my birth certificate while he smoked a cigarette, exhaling the smoke across the desk in my direction.

"What is your destination?" the man behind the desk asked in precise accented English.

"Colonia Juarez."

"And how long will you be there?"

I hesitated. I wasn't sure. Perhaps I didn't care. Colonia Juarez had always held a bit of magic for me, had been a kind of refuge, a place where I could get away from life's distractions and get everything else into focus. There, with Grandma and Grandpa, life was slow-paced and easy with lots of freedom.

While growing up I hadn't gone to Colonia Juarez all that often, maybe once a year at the most; but it was comforting to know that it was there, that if I ever needed an escape it was only a few hours away. Well, I needed an escape. The last place I wanted to be was home in Mesa.

Grandma had invited me to Colonia Juarez, using the phony pretext that Grandpa needed my help during the summer. Of course, I knew Grandpa could hire all the cheap help he needed without taking me on, but when Grandma spoke with me at my homecoming and extended the invitation, I jumped at the chance. I needed some time to myself, away from everything else. Mexico was the best place for that.

I think Mom was torn. She also needed time to herself to sort through the broken pieces of her life. The three girls were making plans to go to Utah for the summer to stay with my Aunt Sharon, but Mom had expected me to stay. I had been away two years on my mission in Brazil. She wanted to get reacquainted and hold onto me a while longer before I left home for good. She really hadn't had a chance to do that during the last three weeks, not with everything crumbling about her and me. I think she would have liked someone to lean on, someone to steady her, but I didn't feel that I could be that person.

Nothing made sense at home, and I had convinced myself there was no reason to stay. Staying was like lying on an operating table wide awake, watching and feeling the doctors open me up and take out a piece at a time. I didn't need that. I didn't want to be a witness to the painful dissembling of my life.

"How long will you be in Colonia Juarez?" the man behind the desk asked again, this time looking up.

"At least for the summer."

The man grabbed the papers for my visa, stuffed them into a huge manual typewriter, and began plunking away at the keys with his two index fingers. Five minutes later I shuffled out of the office and strolled over to Mom and Grandpa, who had waited in the parking lot.

Grandpa never seemed to change. Of course, men like Grandpa never change. He wasn't a huge man, barely six feet; and yet, he loomed large. He was an enigma. He lived in the twentieth century but, dressed in faded Levi's and battered boots, he looked like a nineteenth-century cowboy that had sprouted from the back of a wild horse. He was tall and lanky with big powerful hands and long fingers that were cracked, calloused, and seamed with honest, black dirt. His face was rough and rugged, as though it had been chiseled out of a piece of granite but never really finished and polished. From the eyes down his face was a leathery brown with crow's-feet about his eyes and deep creases in his cheeks. He had piercing blue eyes that peered out from under thick gray bristle brows. His mouth was a hard, thin line and his teeth were big with a gap between the front ones. To look at him a person would never suspect that he was a prominent and prosperous rancher and fruit grower.

"The *aduana*'s already looked over your bags, and I tossed them in the back of the truck."

"Thanks," I managed to mumble, folding my papers and stuffing them into my shirt pocket.

"Well, we better not stand around here," Grandpa announced. "Jacob and I have work to do, and we won't get it done here. It will be pushing dark if we leave now." He turned to Mom, gave her a hug and a kiss on the forehead, and then started toward his off-white Dodge pickup truck.

Mom and I were left facing each other. It was an awkward moment for both of us, one I had dreaded since leaving Mesa, one I would have preferred to have missed. But there was no escaping it now.

I dug my hands into my pockets and shuffled my feet. It was funny how I could suddenly feel like a stranger around my own mother. Throughout my mission I had grown to appreciate my folks more and more. It was easy to express that appreciation and love in letters and tapes. I really had meant to return home, to open up and tell Mom and Dad how wonderful they were and how much I loved them. I had never been able to do that before; but a mission, a little maturity, and a lot of reflection encouraged me to take the risk. Flying home, I rehearsed my expression, but during the first few days home I procrastinated. The time had never been just right, and there was a haze of tension I hadn't been able to identify right off. As a result, I waited, hoping for a more appropriate moment. The moment never came. The sudden crash took its place, and all the sweet intentions turned sour. In a way, I regretted that I had ever contemplated expressing my feelings so openly.

I glanced north, toward the American side. Columbus, New Mexico, was in the distance. Between there and where we stood was the American immigration office with the Stars and Stripes fluttering in front.

"Grandpa and Grandma will take good care of you," Mom encouraged gently, groping for conversation. "They always do." Her voice broke. "And you'll have a better chance to tell them about your mission. They don't always get that opportunity with their other grandchildren."

5

"I'll be all right," I mumbled, kicking at the gravel underfoot.

"The girls and I will miss you."

A bitter smile worked its way onto my lips. "Yeah," I sighed.

"I wish we could have spent more time talking about your mission. I feel like there's so much of it that we — well, that we haven't heard about." She fumbled with the car keys. "But I think . . . well, maybe this will be best," she added, trying to sound cheerful. "Of course, I'm not telling you to go. I'd love to have you stay. But I do understand. And your grandpa is getting older and could use the help."

I nodded.

Mom touched my arm with the tips of her fingers. They trembled just a little. "Good-bye, Jacob. We'll see you . . . in August? I'll try to get a few days off and drive all the way to Colonia Juarez. I'd like to spend some time with Mom and Dad and you. Even if it's just a weekend." She took a step closer, leaned forward, and kissed my cheek. I was a statue of indifference, not because I wanted to be but because I didn't know how not to be.

We were both silent and then I asked, still looking toward the American immigration office half a mile away, "He was excommunicated Tuesday night, wasn't he?"

There was no answer.

"I have a right to know."

"Jacob," Mom whispered, looking about, "I'm not sure that now is the time to — "

"I ought to know if my own father was excommunicated," I cut her short. "There have been too many secrets already."

"Yes," came Mom's quick, quiet reply. "Yes, he was."

I had suspected as much, but still it hurt to hear my suspicions verified. I could have even forgiven Dad for that. But I wasn't sure I could ever forgive him for not coming to tell me good-bye this morning. It was true that he was working a twenty-four-hour shift, but he could have broken away had he

6

really wanted to. He had fumbled through a sort of good-bye the afternoon before while I was packing.

"I wish I could go with you, Jacob," he had said awkwardly, leaning against the doorjamb and looking into my room. "I'd like to take a few days off, head up in the mountains around García, and do some camping. You've never been to Colonia García, have you?" I shook my head. "It's really nice up there. Maybe I'll be able to break away this summer and drop down to see you. García's nice in the summer."

I nodded as I folded a pair of Levi's and laid them in the suitcase. I tried to remember the last time Dad and I had gone camping. Four, five, maybe six years ago. Oh, he'd talked about it plenty since then, but there was always something else coming up. I had learned to accept that. Besides, I wasn't that crazy about camping. Maybe Dad wasn't either. There had been times when we had camped. Those had been good times. Perhaps Dad's talk of camping now was a simple longing to go back to the way things had once been between us. But when Dad mentioned the camping this time, I felt betrayed. It was all a lie. At best a ridiculous dream. We both knew it, but neither could bring himself to admit it. It was easier to play the charade.

"Well, I'll try to break away to drop by and see you in the morning before you leave," he said, straightening up and backing from the room. "But if I get tied up — you know how work is at the fire department — have a good trip. Tell Grandpa and Grandma hello."

I knew he would never show. I knew it even while he was saying he might. And yet, I looked for him the next morning. Even as we were pulling out of the driveway and the betrayal and abandonment became obvious, I continued to look for him. Actually I didn't care about telling him good-bye. I didn't want to tell him good-bye. The real reason I wanted him there was to walk away from him with a show of complete indifference. I wanted to hurt him one final time — like he had hurt me. But he didn't allow me that satisfaction. He simply didn't show up.

His absence didn't lessen my desire to lash out, though; and in the end it was Mom who received the brunt of my anger, because she was the one who cared enough to be with me.

"Where does that leave the two of you?" I asked Mom, unable to keep the bitterness from my voice.

Mom didn't answer.

"Look, Mom," I demanded, my voice rising, "I'm not a lousy kid that doesn't know the facts of life. I'm twenty-one, an adult. I understand why you tried to keep it all from me while I was on my mission. But there isn't a reason anymore. What's going to happen?"

"I don't know, Jacob."

"You don't know, or you won't say?"

Mom raked her fingers through her short brown hair. She had always been pretty, looking ten years younger than her thirty-nine years. My friends used to kid me that I was the only guy around with an older sister for a mother. She was just under five-feet-five-inches, athletic, trim and fit. She was an avid jogger. She and Dad used to run in ten-kilometer races several times a year. She had always been vibrantly happy and outgoing, sharing her smiles and laughs with all those around her. But the last months had taken an ugly toll. The young girl beauty was still there but now screened under gray anxiety. "I'm not sure anymore." Her voice broke.

I knew I should let the whole thing drop, but I was angry and hurt. "Dad said he was going to try to work things out."

"He's said a lot of things. For years he's said a lot of things. Jacob, not all of this happened while you were on your mission. There's more to it than you know right now. I've been fighting this battle for a long time."

"But at least he's willing to try." Even when I said it I guessed it wasn't true. He had no more intention of making things work out with Mom than he had of taking me camping, but I argued the point nevertheless. Maybe I couldn't bring myself to admit that Dad was actually walking out on us, that he had already walked out on us. He just hadn't bothered to slam the door loud enough on his way out.

"Didn't he say he was going to forget . . . her?" I couldn't bring myself to give the other woman a name.

"Sometimes I wonder if I can forget."

"You?"

"It's not always easy to forget something like that." She closed her eyes for a moment. "I have wanted to give up for some time, Jacob. I didn't." She dabbed at her eyes. "I wanted you to come home to a—well, to a full family. I wanted it like it used to be, even if it was for a little while. When your Grandma asked you to spend the summer in Mexico helping Grandpa, I thought it was an answer to prayer. I knew I could hold on that long, long enough for you to . . . " She shook her head. "Maybe we were both trying for you. I don't know if I can try anymore, not now that you know."

"Does that mean . . . " I hesitated. "Divorce?" I asked, almost choking on the word.

Mom reached up and brushed away a tear with the tips of her fingers. She swallowed, shrugged, and shook her head. "I don't know, Jacob."

"You must have some idea." I hadn't wanted to get angry, but I could feel hot blood rush to my cheeks. My voice was rising. "Have you just chucked everything?"

"Jacob!" Mom cut in. Though her eyes were filled with tears, there was an edge to her voice. Her tone was steady and commanding. "I just don't know," she stated slowly, deliberately. "I'm not sure of anything. Sometimes I want it to be all over, behind me forever. Other times I cling to the hope that things will work out. Believe me, I didn't want this to happen. Sometimes I blame myself for what has happened. Maybe I could have made things nicer at home." She shook her head. "But I'm not sure that gives your father the right to . . . " She swallowed. "One thing you need to realize, though, is that you're not the only one that's been hurt by all of this. Some of the rest of us hurt, too."

9

I shook my head. "I just keep thinking," I began slowly, "all the time I was in Brazil I thought everything was so . . . so perfect at home." I closed my eyes and then opened them. "But they weren't. It was all a charade."

"Jacob, I suppose you have a right to be angry with me for creating that charade. But remember, I had to live in it. And it wasn't always easy."

"What happens to the girls and me?" I asked, unwilling to let up.

"As you said, you're an adult. You're able to go where you choose."

"And you and Dad fight over the three girls?" I said, staring at Mom. She stared back. All traces of tears were gone. There was anger in her eyes. I knew she had wanted this to be a pleasant farewell, just as she had wanted my homecoming to be happy. But I wasn't in the mood. None of this was fair. I'd served my mission. I'd given it my very best. Everything was supposed to get better while you were on a mission. Your family was supposed to be blessed, develop more unity, grow stronger in the gospel.

I wasn't supposed to come from a broken home! All of that was for those other guys—the lowlifes, the party crowd, the rowdy bunch that had always jammed the parking lot at Mesa High and smoked pot or boozed it up on the weekends. Sure, *their* parents got divorced. Everybody expected that from them. But we were Mormons! My folks had been married in the temple. We'd gone to church. Oh, Mom and Dad had argued occasionally. Dad had had a crazy work schedule with the fire department. We didn't have a perfect family. But we weren't candidates for the broken home rolls. At least I hadn't thought we were, until a couple of weeks ago when I discovered that our family had suddenly crumbled into a heap.

I felt a tightening in the pit of my stomach, and my bitterness festered anew. Though I didn't want to replay the old familiar scene, it forced its way into my thoughts.

I had been home from Brazil a week and a half and had

left the house on a late Thursday afternoon to drive over to a Young Adult party. Halfway to the church I realized I had left my wallet home. Turning around, I drove back to the house, slipped in the side door, and went to my room in the basement. The three girls were visiting friends, so Mom and Dad assumed they were alone.

Even before I could understand what they were saying, I knew something was terribly wrong. They were talking loudly, just a few decibels under a yell. I had heard them raise their voices before, but this was different, and suddenly I began to understand the baffling tension I had sensed since coming home from Brazil.

Mom was crying. Dad was pacing and trying to reason everything into a logical, acceptable explanation. I hadn't meant to eavesdrop. I was just there, listening to my world fall apart.

As I stood next to Mom in the border parking lot, I closed my eyes tight, so tight that yellow lights burst in the blackness, dug my fingernails into the palms of my hands, and choked back the rage. Dad was just going to walk out on us. He'd met someone else, somebody named Liz Carroll. She wasn't even a member. He'd been seeing her off and on for nearly two years. All that time he had been living a loathsome lie.

I didn't go to the Young Adult party. I crept back to my bed, lay in the deepening blackness, and tried to tell myself that it was all a horrible dream. Dad wasn't perfect. I knew that. But he wouldn't run off with another woman. Would he?

At first I hurt. Then slowly the hurt hardened into hate. Yes, I think I hated my dad. He didn't deserve my love or have any claim to my respect. Because of him I felt like dirt, like some kind of bastard, and the thing that was so frustrating was that none of it was my fault. Someone else had messed up my whole life, and I didn't even have a say in it.

It was that Thursday evening that I decided to go to Mexico. I wanted to be as far from home as I could get.

"I didn't want things to be like this," Mom said, breaking into my thoughts. "I think I've tried."

"Well, I guess it doesn't make much difference anymore. Everything's messed up good and royal just the same," I muttered, turning for Grandpa's truck.

"Jacob," Mom called after me.

I stopped without turning around to face her.

"Jacob," Mom started haltingly. I could hear her feet crunch on the gravel as she came up behind me. I knew she was close enough to touch me, but she didn't. "Jacob," she whispered. The cool sternness had melted from her voice. I could tell she was crying. "I've never been good about expressing my feelings. Even to your dad. Maybe that was a lot of the problem." There was a pause and then a muffled sniffle. "I do love you, Jacob. I know I haven't told you that enough, but it's true. In so many ways you and the girls are all I have left. I don't want to lose any of you. You don't have to go."

I can remember thinking that I should turn and say something, reciprocate in some way. I felt guilty leaving Mom. Deep down I knew she needed me, was even hoping that I would change my mind and return to Mesa with her. My mind was made up, though. I could have turned and kissed her without saying a word, but I didn't. I didn't even nod my head to acknowledge her expression. I simply stood there another moment and then headed for the truck and climbed in. I would have preferred to have done that to Dad, but under the circumstances Mom had to do.

As Grandpa started the engine and drove away, I didn't look back. I'm not sure why I didn't. Perhaps it was an attempt to punish Dad through Mom. Maybe I didn't want to admit that I still loved someone who had allowed my world to crumble. Maybe I was afraid of what I might see. To this day I'm convinced that Mom stood there in the parking lot at the immigration office staring down the road until we finally drove out of sight.

# Chapter Two

It was midafternoon as Grandpa and I drove down Palomas's dusty, rutted main street. Except for an occasional housewife standing in her front door and fanning herself in an attempt to find some relief from the oppressive heat, the street was deserted.

"I've seen warmer farewells," Grandpa remarked, accelerating at the edge of town.

"I'm not big on farewells," I muttered. "At least not that kind." Still simmering, I looked out the window, squinting against the sun's glare. Bitterness and guilt rested in my craw like a hard, hot lump.

From Palomas to Concepción, fifty miles away, we drove in silence without so much as a comment about the weather. I stared at the countryside passing in a blur, but saw nothing. I was blind to the present; my mind was entangled in the past.

Mom's and Dad's problems had shaken more than the foundation of my family. My faith had felt tremors as well. I had always been led to believe that if you lived a decent life, you got a decent return on your investment. And I'd lived all right. I wasn't lily-white; and yet, I figured I was better than most. I'd graduated from seminary. I'd earned my Duty to God award. I'd served a mission, even been assistant to the president. I'd never partied. But where had it gotten me? I had ended up from a broken home. It wasn't fair. I got to thinking that maybe it didn't really matter what you did. Life was going to throw you a curve anyway. If living right couldn't at least bring you a decent family, what was the sense of even trying?

There was one thing that gave me hope, prevented me from giving up completely. I had a friend whose parents had divorced. They'd gone their separate ways for three years, but had then gotten back together and even been sealed in the temple. To look at them now, you'd never suspect that they had ever disagreed. I clung to the farfetched notion that Mom and Dad would work out their differences and at the end of the summer I'd return to Mesa and things would be back to normal.

As we drove through the streets of Concepción, halfway to Colonia Juarez, Grandpa groaned and asked, "You feeling better now?"

I shrugged.

"Your grandma and I have been looking forward to your coming. It will be like the old days when you came down for a long stretch in the summer."

I didn't answer.

"There was a time when you liked coming down here."

I nodded. When I was younger a summer had seldom passed that I didn't spend at least four or five weeks of it with Grandpa and Grandma. But later Scouts, friends, and summer jobs had squeezed Mexico out of my summer schedule. It was hard to believe it had been eight years since I spent a summer in Mexico.

"I was hoping you'd be more excited about coming. You look like you're on your way to prison."

I smiled. "I'm glad to be here, Grandpa. Next to Brazil, I'd rather be in Mexico than any other place." I shook my head. "I just hadn't counted on things being like . . . " I pressed my lips together. "Ever since," I paused and cleared my throat, "since finding out everything, I've wanted to come here."

"I'm sure there are easier places in Mesa to make a buck," Grandpa chuckled, "but—"

"It's not the money, Grandpa."

"I'll make it right with you. I can use the help, and—"

"It's not that, Grandpa. I'm glad to be here. It's just that—well, I wish I were here for a different reason."

"I sort of got that impression at the border."

I looked out the window. The ride from Palomas to Concepción had given my anger time to dissipate. "It's nothing personal, though. It doesn't have anything to do with you and Grandma. I just couldn't stay there. Not with things the way they are. I don't want to live with somebody else's mess-up."

"Life's full of mess-ups. Sometimes you have to adjust to other people's mistakes." Grandpa looked over at me and grinned. "I don't know what kind of an adjustment you'll get down here, but I'm planning to work your tail off. I sure as heck aim to get my money's worth."

I smiled. "I'm not a kid anymore. I might work you into the ground, Grandpa."

"Don't let the wrinkles and limp fool you. On your best day and my worst—" A hoarse chuckle rumbled in his chest. "You've spent the last two years rapping your knuckles on doors. But we'll put some calluses on the palms of your hands. We'll make a real man out of you."

I laughed, suddenly feeling better. I wasn't one to have heroes, but Grandpa came the closest to any I knew. He was something of a living legend. He could tell all kinds of stories about hunting, ranching, going on cattle drives, being lost for days in the mountains, facing angry mobs, fighting bullies. The list could go on. And everything Grandpa talked about came from personal experience.

When he was eighteen, he and his older brother Harold had been gunned down by a bunch of angry Mexicans. Harold had died. Grandpa had lived—barely. I didn't know all that had happened. Grandpa seldom talked about it, so the details were vague. But that didn't prevent my imagination from filling in the gaps. Ever since I was a kid, I had concluded that, by virtue of his being shot down and surviving, Grandpa was as illustrious and famous as Billy the Kid, Wyatt Earp, or any other western hero.

"Mom says it's different in the colonies now," I remarked, warming up to Grandpa and wanting to forget home.

"Yeah," Grandpa answered with a touch of sorrow. "You know how the bottom's fallen out of the economy. When you used to visit here, the peso's exchange was between twelve and twenty-six to the dollar. It's hitting over seven hundred now. There's talk of it going to a thousand before the end of the year." He sighed. "I don't know where it's going to end. Workers are threatening to strike. The agrarians are stirring up trouble."

"The agrarians?" I asked. "Aren't they the ones that move onto the ranchers' lands?"

Grandpa nodded. "They just move in and set up camp. They claim the land for themselves and hope no one pushes them off. A few years back a group moved onto the Whettens' ranch. They were there several months."

"Couldn't the Whettens do anything?"

"Oh, we did what we could. It was a community problem, so all the ranchers tried to work together. We went to Chihuahua City many times and pleaded our case to a lot of people there. We even went to the governor."

"And nothing worked?"

"After a lot of waiting and worrying, one day two trucks loaded with troops drove out to the Whettens' ranch, backed their trucks up to the agrarian camp, uncovered a machine gun, and ordered the agrarians out."

"Well, that's one way to deal with trespassers," I mused. "And now they're back?"

"Walt Shupe figures there's a group ready to move onto his place. At least those are the rumors floating around."

"Can't Shupe just drive them off before they get settled? Can't he go to the police or something?"

"The battle for land has been going on for hundreds of years in Mexico. Mexico's last big revolution, between 1912

16

and 1920, was supposed to have equalized everything. But it didn't. Most of the old problems remain. The rich still live off the poor.

"The agrarians figure that they might succeed in getting a chunk of land if they move onto the Mormons' ranches. Agrarians in other places have gotten away with it. With the economy so bad there are more and more agrarians willing to take that gamble."

I glanced over at Grandpa. He was staring straight ahead, his jaw set solidly and both hands gripping the wheel. "And so you think all of that land grabbing will start up in Colonia Juarez?"

"It's possible, Jacob. Even probable."

We passed through Janos, a small town forty miles from Nuevo Casas Grandes. It was nothing more than a motley collection of adobe houses and an ancient Catholic church off to the right. From Janos we raced on to Dublán, the other Mormon colony still in Mexico; then we entered Nuevo Casas Grandes, a city of about forty thousand people.

When we reached Casas, as it was known by most in the colonies, the sun was setting and the cool of evening was upon us. The streets were filling with people; and the blare of horns, the rattle of old trucks, and the scream of mariachi music was everywhere. As we approached the main plaza, I could see the crowds gathering. The shoeshine boys were out in force along with the kids selling gum and candy. Older men pushing *paleta* carts weaved in and out of the streams of people, selling their ice cream and ice bars. Suddenly a flood of memories returned. I felt excited to be back in Mexico. I sat up and looked down one of the familiar streets. "Is the old *paleta* store still open, the one that sells the big fruit *paletas* for six pesos?"

Grandpa laughed. "Yeah, the store's still there, but the *paletas* are going for two hundred pesos. I told you things were different."

I squirmed with excitement as we passed through Casas.

17

It had been eight years since I'd driven through the city. I wanted to see everything.

"What's going on there?" I gasped as we approached the huge Paquimé fruit complex where most of the Mormon fruit growers sent their fruit to be packed and shipped all over Mexico. "Are they having a war or something?"

I stared at the men dressed in pale blue uniforms and stationed all about the high cement walls of the Paquimé plant. "Some of those guys are packing submachine guns. Are they for real?"

"They're for real," Grandpa responded grimly. "Some of the workers are trying to start a strike. The state police were sent in to make sure there wasn't any trouble."

"They don't mess around, do they?" I asked as we passed the plant's front gate and saw several state policemen posted there with guns slung over their shoulders.

"Like I said, Mexico is changing. Things are tense. There are a lot of folks looking for work. The ones already working figure their wages ought to be raised, but if anyone strikes somebody else will be in there the next day to take their place." He shook his head sadly. "As long as the state police are here, the strike won't happen."

"Dang!" I exclaimed as we drove by slowly and a group of gun-toting policemen looked our way. "This looks like a war zone."

"I don't know how most of these people make it," Grandpa sighed heavily. "If something isn't done soon, the lid's going to blow off Mexico. When the people get hungry enough, it's not going to matter how many state policemen they send for."

Casas, bursting with life and teaming with tension, was soon left behind as we made our way to Colonia Juarez. I slumped down in my seat and gazed out the window, watching the last fourteen miles flash by.

Colonia Juarez is nestled in a quaint green valley surrounded by brown, rolling hills. The Piedras Verdes River trickles down through the valley and divides the town itself.

A one-lane bridge spans the river and connects the east side of town to the west. On the east side of the river are the Catholic Church and the town store, La Sorpresa. The post office is down the street, an ancient structure with barred windows and cracked walls, looking like something out of the last century. On the west side of the river is the Mormon chapel with its lofty spire piercing the clear air and its well-kept lawns and shrubbery. South of the church is Academia Juarez, the Church academy. Colonia Juarez appears to have been lifted from some small western community and plopped down in the middle of this northern Mexico countryside.

Grandpa drove over the last hill, and as we started down the steep dugway that dropped into the valley, the green of Colonia Juarez greeted me. In the growing dusk, I could see the verdant orchards stretching everywhere, and the old excitement returned. Though I would have been slow to admit it to anyone just then, I was glad to be in Colonia Juarez. As long as I was looking for a refuge, I was satisfied to come here, where for an entire summer I wouldn't be a witness to my family's fall.

# Chapter Three

Just after five-thirty the next morning, I was awakened by the low growl of truck engines and the murmer of men's voices outside my open window. Then I heard the crunch of boots on loose gravel as someone trudged up the walk to the kitchen door and knocked lightly. I pushed myself into a sitting position on the edge of the bed, scratching my head and rubbing my eyes, and stared bleary-eyed about the bedroom. In the gray shadows I spotted my suitcase in the corner, still packed. My shirt and pants were flung over the only chair in the room, where I had tossed them before crashing into bed the night before. Slowly I recalled where I was.

"Hello, Jake," a man greeted Grandpa. The man's tone was grave, guarded.

"Come in, Calvin," I heard Grandpa invite. "What brings you out this time of the morning?"

The man coughed. "Why don't you walk out to the truck. Some of the others are here, too. We won't wake your wife that way."

As the man and Grandpa made their way down the gravel walk, I strained to listen, staring toward the window where blue cotton curtains stirred as an early-morning breeze breathed through the screen. "The agrarians made their move. I knew they would."

"Walt Shupe's place?"

"Sometime yesterday. Thirty, maybe forty of them. I'd say there are close to a dozen families."

Grandpa and the man stopped a few feet from my open window. "Are you sure?" Grandpa asked. "I mean, you're sure they're not just passing through. Maybe heading for the mountains?"

"Not a chance. Walt sent word in with his son Clyde not more than thirty minutes ago. They didn't dare come last night with the agrarians so close. The agrarians cut through two different fences, tore out the posts, used them for firewood. They're setting up shop, Jake. Clyde wasn't sure, but he figured they grabbed one of their cows, too." There was a moment's silence, and then the man continued. "Jake, this group is as bold as you please. You know where that windmill and water hole of Walt's is just north of his house?"

"That's less than two miles from his house."

"That's where they are. They're using his well, driving his cattle away." There was another pause. "Jake, if they can get away with this, others will get bold and move out there, too. We can't let them stay. Even for a day or so. It's Shupe's place today. But tomorrow . . ." He left the sentence unfinished.

"I've been expecting something like this," I heard Grandpa say. "Not quite so many. And not all at once."

"We've got to move them off, Jake."

"Any suggestions, Calvin?"

The other man hesitated. "Maybe it's time we got a little — rough."

There was grumbled approval from several others.

"What about going to Chihuahua City?"

The man laughed humorlessly. "We can't just wait around until Chihuahua decides to do something."

"It worked the last time."

"But it took them six months to send the troops," someone else spoke up. "Give this gang six months and they'll have houses and gardens out there."

22

"And that was six years ago," Calvin added. "It's different this time around. The peso wasn't going seven hundred to one against the dollar. If we wait as long this time, we're going to have squatters all over our range. And if very many of them move out there, it's going to take more than a truckload of troops to send them packing. By then the governor will find the problem too sticky to do anything about it. It will just be easier to look the other way and let us gringos eat the loss. We've got to move, Jake."

"What are you suggesting?"

"We still outnumber them. We can go out there and throw them off. There was a time when you were willing to use force, Jake. If you had to."

I grew tense, straining to hear every word. There was a dry chuckle. I wasn't sure whose it was until it faded and Grandpa spoke. "Force has a way of blowing up in your face."

"It's our land, Jake."

"It could be your life, Calvin. Those agrarians aren't the only ones that can get hurt if things get out of hand. I've had a little experience myself along those lines."

"Nobody's forgotten you and Harold."

"I wasn't necessarily thinking of Harold. There have been others. Before and after."

"Look, Jake," Calvin protested, "that land's been bought and paid for several times over, just like some of yours has. Maybe it's time we stopped playing the nice guy. We've paid all the fees and *mordidas* that can be expected. If we don't move now, we might never have another chance."

"I still say our best bet is to pursue a legal course in Chihuahua City. Even if we have to park on the governor's doorstep. I know it's slow. But we know it works."

"What's wrong with just taking back what's ours?" Calvin asked.

"We start pushing our weight around, roughing people up, especially poor people, who in the eyes of many are just trying to scratch a simple living out of the soil—Mexican soil—and

23

we'll likely find that we've got more of a revolt out in this valley than we know what to do with. Maybe then the agrarians will find a reason to go to the governor. The next time the troops drive out here, they might be asking *us* to leave."

"This is our land, Jake."

"It was our land in 1912, too. But when push came to shove, it was the Mormons who packed their bags."

"We're not in the middle of a revolution this time, Jake."

"No?" Grandpa chuckled dryly. "This whole country's ready to bust open, from one end to the other. Drive past the Paquimé plant and tell me there's not a revolution. Pancho Villa isn't riding this time, but inflation, unemployment, strikes, dirt-level poverty are mean substitutes. In a lot of people's eyes we're still foreigners. And you know how Mexicans feel about foreigners."

"I'm not going to lose my land to a bunch of dirty squatters."

"It wouldn't be the first time a rancher lost his land, Calvin. Being Anglo, we've already got two strikes against us. We better be careful how we take this next pitch, because we only have one swing. And the last thing we need is to get thrown out of the game altogether."

"That range land isn't even fit for farming," Calvin argued. "There's not enough water out there to farm. You can run cattle out there, but it's not good for much else. Those squatters will find that out soon enough. But by then the range won't be any good to anybody. We won't even be able to run cattle on it. I'm not losing my land, Jake. Even if I have to fight for it. Now you can stand with us or—"

"If we're going to win this battle, Calvin," Grandpa cut in, "we're going to all have to stand together. This isn't an individual fight. This involves all of us. When we move, we have to move together. Maybe when push comes to shove it will mean a fight. Right now I suggest we keep our heads and not rush out there and do something rash. Has anybody even talked to those fellows out there?"

24

"You can't reason with people like that, Jake."

"We can always start a fight, Calvin. But right now might be the only time when we can talk. I suggest we do it."

"You're too much of a bleeding heart these days, Jake. We can't always be on the giving end or sooner or later we end up with nothing left to give."

"I'm not talking about giving anything. All I want is to talk to them."

"I don't want to lose my land," another man spoke. "I say we do it Jake's way, though."

There was a mumble of agreement.

"Do the rest of you feel that way?" Calvin questioned. There was no audible reply, but then Calvin heaved a sigh and conceded, "All right, we'll meet back here in an hour or so. And we'll talk to them."

I was dressed within minutes and tiptoeing barefoot down the hall to the kitchen. Grandma wasn't up yet. The house was quiet. I dropped onto a kitchen chair, pulled on my shoes, and then slipped out the side door in search of Grandpa.

I paused just outside the kitchen and looked about. The night before I hadn't had a chance to take a good look at the place. Grandpa's house was a two-story, dark brick house with two gables in front and thick Virginia creepers covering the west side. It was set back fifty yards from the unpaved street and surrounded by a huge lawn in front and a small garden in back, all of which was enclosed within a four-foot-high chain link fence. Flower gardens, rosebushes, and shrubbery were scattered about, all products of Grandma's pride and patience.

To the south of the house were the machinery sheds, the barn, the haystacks, and a corral. Leading from the barn area to the house was a narrow gravel path that wound its way through grapevines and berry bushes to a side door and Grandma's kitchen.

The home was a modest one. Uncle Travis, Grandpa's only son and the one who worked closely with him in his ranching and orchard business, owned a huge rambling ranch house on a hill west of town. Grandpa could have afforded something as grand, but he was content to live in his three-bedroom home, the one he had built forty years earlier when he had been less prosperous.

I found Grandpa behind the barn throwing hay down to a half dozen calves. He didn't hear me approach.

"Can I go, too?" I burst out.

Grandpa glanced in my direction. "You're up early." He brushed hay leaves from his pants, snatched up a grain bucket, and headed for the barn. "I wasn't expecting you until the middle of the morning. You had a long day yesterday."

"I woke up early," I explained. "Can I go with you?"

"Where?"

"To see the squatters?"

Grandpa stopped and turned around.

"You were right outside my window," I said, shrugging. "I couldn't help but hear."

Grandpa studied me for a moment without answering.

"I'm not a kid, Grandpa," I protested.

"It doesn't have anything to do with being a kid," Grandpa muttered as he turned and entered the barn. "You act like you're going out to see a circus act." I followed him into the dark interior of the barn. The smell of alfalfa, grain, and leather was heavy. "If I'm going to be here this summer," I continued, "don't I at least have the right to know what's going on?"

Grandpa walked past me and headed back to the corral. I followed him. He emptied the grain bucket into a wooden grain box and watched as the year-old calves crowded forward, bunting each other and pushing their noses into the yellow grain. "I'm not sure it's a proper place for you. I brought you down to work for me — not throw you into the first fight that came along."

"I can take care of myself. I know a thing or two about fighting."

Grandpa took a deep breath, hung the bucket on a post,

26

and leaned against the fence. "Do you know anything about talking? We have plenty that want a fight."

"Someone can come along and just walk away with your land? And you can't do anything about it? I know Mexico is different, but —"

"Mexico is unpredictable. The law . . . " Grandpa shook his head. "Sometimes the law is as much convenience as anything. If the masses are relatively content, then nobody in the government worries too much. But when the masses become restless, the government gets uneasy and looks for ways to appease the people.

"It's like a parent with a bawling child. Most of the time the parent can just let the child howl and carry on. But if that bawling goes on very long, the parent gets nervous and begins looking for ways to quiet the child down. He'll shove a cookie or a sucker in the child's mouth and hope that will calm him down. Well, Mexico has been bawling for a long time. There are people in government who take the attitude that the masses have always bawled and complained and there's nothing to worry about. But there are others who are getting nervous. They can see that the bawling is getting louder and more demanding. They're looking for a cracker to toss to this big bawling kid, because if this big bawling kid ever decides to fix what's bothering him, the people in government will be the first to go."

"And the cracker for this bawling child is your land?" I asked.

"It's not just the land here. If the government looks the other way when the masses snatch a bit of land from the rich, no harm is done. The government can live with the whine from a handful of rich folks if it quiets the roar from the masses."

"The Shupes are rich?"

Grandpa shook his head. "Not really. Walt struggles to make ends meet like any other rancher. The fall of the peso has been hard on him too. Of course, Shupe's better off than

27

those agrarians out there, and that's the only thing those agrarians think about. They don't see a man sweating over his books to make them balance; they just look at all that land and figure that it's more than any one man really needs."

"So Shupe's going to lose his land just because the government doesn't want the masses to get too rowdy?"

"This isn't the first time the folks in the colonies have been through this. It won't be the last. The Mormons have been fighting this battle over land ever since they came in 1885. They got run out of the States because of polygamy. The Church sent them to Mexico so they could live without being harassed by the federal marshals. The folks that settled Juarez settled on a piece of land further down the river from where Juarez is right now. Down by Cuautemoch. They'd been led to believe that was the land they'd bought. They built their homes, plowed their fields, planted their trees, put up their barns and corrals — only to learn a while later that they were on the wrong section of land. They had to start all over again here in Juarez. And they prospered. Nobody else wanted this land. The Mormons built their brick homes, dug their wells, made their sawmills, ground their flour, and did a hundred other things that had never been done here before. That's when people got a little envious.

"Then the revolution came. Pancho Villa and his gang stormed through on a rampage, taking what they wanted. The *Federales* followed, snatching up what they wanted. Common bandits demanded their share. It wasn't long before the Mormons didn't have a choice. Either they left or they stayed and got robbed and murdered.

"After the revolution, most of the Mormons stayed in the States. They had already started over in Arizona, New Mexico, and Texas, and there was no reason to pull up roots and return to Mexico. But a few Mormons came back and started over again. This was their land. They loved it. They were proud of it. It was paid for. But there were always those who coveted what the Mormons had. In their minds the Mormons were foreigners, not entitled to anything. It didn't matter that these Mormons were Mexicans, born and raised here and loyal to this country. Unfortunately, they were white. That seemed to make all the difference.

"So over the years the Mormons have struggled to keep what was legally theirs. We've been to visit nearly every governor of the state of Chihuahua since the revolution. We've paid for lawyers. We've paid *mordidas* and hidden fees and everything else. That's why most of the ranchers and fruit growers around here have paid for their places several times over. And they'll probably keep right on paying."

"If you've been messed over so many times," I asked, "why don't you stand up and drive those squatters off like Calvin wants to do?"

"Never act rash, Jacob."

"Rash?" I grumbled. "Saving your own land is rash?"

"Seventy years ago, when Villa was knocking at the door, there were those who wanted to stay and fight, make a last-ditch stand. Right was on their side." Grandpa paused and glanced over at me. "If that had happened, there wouldn't be a Mormon colony in Mexico right now. No Mormon would have ever been allowed back into Mexico. We would have been finished here. Forever!"

"But," I argued, "if these agrarians keep coming, you won't have anything anyway."

Grandpa shrugged. "There were a lot of people who thought the Mormon colonies were finished when Villa drove the Mormons out, but the colonies survived. There are a lot of prophets of doom saying that the squatters, the inflation, the unemployment and all the other problems facing Mexico will squeeze the colonies out of existence." Grandpa shrugged again. "Maybe. But if we're careful, if we don't do anything rash, we'll survive. We'll be different. But maybe better."

"Have you ever considered leaving Mexico?"

Grandpa chuckled and shook his head.

"You could go to the States. Nothing like this would happen there. Why, if somebody moved onto your land out there—"

"I don't have any land in the States, Jacob," Grandpa interrupted, smiling. "And do you know of anybody up that way looking for an old man, past retirement age, who knows how to ranch?" He shook his head. "I could never work for another man. I've been my own boss too long. Mexico has her problems, but she's home. I have to make the best of it. And I can still love her."

# Chapter Four

Breakfast was a quiet occasion, so different from dinner the night before when Grandma had encouraged me to talk nonstop, trying to get caught up on all the news from home. From the moment she pulled me from the truck, threw her arms around my neck, and gave me a kiss, she had kept me talking. My dinner was cold before I had a chance to eat.

At first I was reluctant to open up. I didn't want to discuss Mom and Dad and their troubles. I was afraid Grandma would intrude into those sensitive areas. But she was careful to steer the conversation away from anything potentially painful. Within minutes she helped me forget that my visit to Colonia Juarez was an escape.

Unlike Grandpa, Grandma was talkative, vivacious and outgoing, bubbling with life. Her eyes were dark, almost black, and sparkled with enthusiasm. She was several inches shorter than Grandpa, narrow in the waist, and had small feet and delicate hands. The years had frosted her once black hair and left traces of wrinkles about her eyes and mouth, but not even age could extinguish her youthful glow. Her captivating smile was as much a part of her as Grandpa's unshaven chin and weather-burned features were a part of him. In many ways she was a contrast to the rough, unpolished man she had married. And yet, the two complemented each other in a strange kind of way.

"You are certainly up early," Grandma observed, breaking the silence that had prevailed during the first half of breakfast. "I thought you'd sleep in. Before your grandpa puts you to work." She smiled. "He's been known to work guests just like hired hands. But for less pay." Her eyes twinkled as she poured me some more milk.

"I'm ready." I glanced over at Grandpa. He crunched down on a piece of toast and reached for the last slice of bacon on the plate.

"What do you have planned for today?" Grandma questioned.

Grandpa hesitated for a moment. "I need to run out to the—" He cleared his throat. "Calvin Cramer wants me to ride out with him."

"So the agrarians moved onto the Shupe place," Grandma stated matter-of-factly.

Grandpa continued to chew his bacon. He looked across the table at me and then glanced at Grandma. "Were you listening at your window, too?"

"It's not often that Calvin Cramer stops by for a social call at 5:30 A.M. Besides, I've known it was coming." She stood and began clearing the table. "What are you going to do?"

"Talk."

"Will talk do any good?"

"No."

"Then why not do it Calvin's way?" I burst out.

"Talk buys us time. Before we wade into this fight, we'd better know why we're fighting."

"For your land."

Grandpa finished his water and shook his head. "It's not that simple. It never is." He started for the door. "You coming?" he asked over his shoulder.

"Can I?" I wet my lips. "I mean, I didn't think—"

"Just remember that we're not going to an exhibit at the zoo. This isn't Mesa, Arizona."

32

There were eight of us in the three trucks that drove toward the Shupes' ranch. Grandpa and I went in his truck. It was a quiet ride. Neither of us spoke.

We bounced and lurched over a rough rocky road that wound up past the Romneys' orchards. Our little caravan crawled out of Juarez's green valley and onto the dry flats between the town and the mountains several miles in the distance. The country was dry and sandy, spotted by faded clumps of grass, sagebrush, and yucca plants.

I stared across the flats, straining to catch the first glimpse of the camp. At that point it still hadn't occurred to me that this was anything very serious. My sheltered realm of reality didn't include range wars and hostilities. I saw this as an adventurous jaunt that would be good for a few moments of excitement. Then Grandpa and I would return to the business of ranching and orchard work.

After driving for twenty minutes we met Clyde Shupe, a kid not more than a couple years younger than I. He was pacing back and forth next to his light blue pickup truck. His tanned, narrow face was tense, and he gripped a rifle in his hand.

Grandpa stopped his truck, leaned out the window, and spoke to Clyde. "Anything happen?"

Clyde rubbed his mouth nervously with the back of his hand and looked out across the flats. I followed his gaze. In the distance I spotted several buildings and sheds, all with tin roofs. To the right of the buildings were some corrals with a windmill in the middle. "You can see them from our place if you climb up on the windmill," Clyde explained. He swallowed and pointed to the west. "They're camping in a little dip over that way. We can't figure them out. Dad's afraid to leave the place for fear they'll sneak in and steal something. He sent me out here to wait for you."

Grandpa glanced down at Clyde's rifle. "We probably won't need that."

Clyde gripped the gun more tightly. "I've got it if I need it."

33

"You don't need it right now. Put it up."

Clyde hesitated a moment and then slowly set the rifle on the seat of his truck.

"Well, Jake, where do we go from here?" Calvin Cramer asked, stepping next to Clyde and surveying the country before him. Calvin was a big, powerful man, probably six-foot-four. He had thick shoulders, a huge chest, and a bit of a potbelly that sagged over and strained at his belt buckle. His face was round and filled out; but, like all the other men in Juarez, it was tanned from his eyes down. He pulled his hat off to wipe his brow. I noticed that he was balding fast.

"You still figure we should talk?" Calvin asked Grandpa.

Grandpa nodded.

"Then you're probably the best man for the job."

When we reached the agrarian camp, we found six or seven makeshift tents — basically worn, moth-eaten tarps thrown over poles and staked down with rusty spikes and strands of twine. Three cooking fires were scattered about the camp with blackened pots hanging over them. I couldn't see more than a couple dozen people in the camp itself, most of whom were women and kids. Beyond the windmill and water tank several men were urging two mule teams back and forth across a dusty patch of bare earth that was supposed to be a field. Others chopped at brush, and others lugged rocks. There were two ancient, battered flatbed trucks parked by the windmill. They were so old I couldn't tell what model they were. The rusted hood was up on the one; the other sagged at the rear because of a flat tire.

I'm not sure what I had expected. Definitely not real people, people covered with dirt and staggering under the burden of poverty, a kind of poverty I'd never witnessed outside of Brazil. When I had heard Grandpa and Calvin speak of the agrarians, they had been nameless, faceless thieves. Now I was sickened a little by the conditions I saw. These were real people, the same kinds of people I had preached the gospel to in Brazil.

The women and children crowded about the tents and

34

stared in our direction, their eyes wide, curious and fearful. From within one of the tents came the wail of a baby.

The men wandered into the camp and formed a silent, sullen wall. Their eyes were dark and full of suspicious curiosity. They seemed lost, groping in a dazed state, staring at us as though we were something from another world.

Grandpa opened his door and stepped from the truck. I proceeded to do likewise, but before I could step from the truck Grandpa stopped me short.

"Jacob," Grandpa spoke. His voice was low, sudden and final. "Stay in the truck." All morning he had seemed imperturbable; now his voice betrayed him.

"*Buenos dias*," Grandpa greeted. The tension was suddenly gone from his voice. He even managed to smile.

The men before him didn't answer or even nod their heads in acknowledgment. The other men from Juarez climbed from their trucks but didn't move in. Grandpa looked about the camp, surveying it carefully. His gaze settled on one battered tent where a man rested on his haunches just inside the open flap. He stared for a moment and then glanced toward the water tank where the Shupes' windmill whirred steadily overhead. At the base of the windmill stood another man.

Turning back to the men in front of him, Grandpa began to speak. One of the squatters, a wiry man in his early thirties, acted as the spokesman.

I had learned Portuguese on my mission so I could pick out a few words and phrases. But I couldn't keep up with the quick Spanish Grandpa and the squatter used. The squatter's tone, his hand gestures, his taunting grin, left no doubt as to what he was saying. After several minutes of discussion, Grandpa nodded his head once and concluded with a resigned, "*Bueno, nos vemos.*"

The man grinned and remarked, "*Les esperamos.*"

"Well, that's what we get for talking," Calvin Cramer muttered as Grandpa ambled back to the truck.

"There's no hurry yet, Calvin."

35

"Come on, Jake, you heard what he said. They're not moving. Before next week they'll be building out here. It might just be cardboard shacks, but it will be home to them."

"What do you propose?"

Calvin Cramer cleared his throat and scratched the back of his neck. "I say we load up this camp right now. Just throw their stuff on our trucks and haul everything out of here, every pot, every spoon, every last blanket. We'll tell them they can pick up their stuff in Juarez. If they don't pick it up by tonight, we'll take it over to the dump and burn it. We can move this camp out of here in thirty minutes easy."

"And maybe these agrarians will help us load it up," Grandpa remarked.

"There are nine of us, counting the Shupe boy and your Jacob." Calvin swallowed and rubbed his chin with the back of his hand. "They're not going to fight the whole bunch of us."

There was a suffocating silence. Grandpa turned back and faced the squatters who were watching our every move, suspicious of our discussion in English. "Jacob," Grandpa said to me without turning around, "you'd better close your door."

"But, Grandpa, I can —"

"Jacob," Grandpa cut me off, his voice like a hot knife slashing through my protest.

"Are you leading the charge, Calvin?" Grandpa asked.

I waited, hardly breathing. My mouth was dry, the palms of my hands were damp, my fingers twitched.

"I figure there's probably a better time," Milton Whetten, a small wiry man in his early forties, croaked. "They're ready for us now. There's no sense in starting something we can't finish."

"I'm with Jake," agreed Preston Call, a younger man. "We can head back and plan something else. We don't have to jump into the middle of this right now."

"What do you mean by backing out?" Clyde Shupe blurted, turning on the other ranchers, all of whom were years older than he. "I thought you came out here to help drive them out.

36

And now you want to run back to town with your tails between your legs. We've got to do something! Now!"

His face was red with rage. I felt sorry for him. He was right. We should help him. These people were a bunch of thugs. Any pity I had felt for them earlier was suddenly gone. Their poverty didn't give them a right to steal.

"Clyde," Grandpa said, taking him by the arm just above the elbow. "We're not leaving you alone. We're going to help you to—"

"Get your hands off me," he protested, shaking his arm free. He glared at Grandpa and then back at the others. "Sure you can run back to town and do some more planning. They're not parked on your land. I came to clean this camp out, and I intend to do it. This is Shupe land."

He turned and charged toward the camp. He kicked a pot from the first fire and then lunged for the nearest tent, ripping out the corner stake and pulling the tarp back. As he did, two shots boomed, the bullets kicking up dust no more than six inches from Clyde's feet. He whipped around and tripped backward over a tent stake, landing on his back. There was a tense moment of silence. Then Clyde scrambled to his feet to continue his rampage, but as he did another shot thundered and the bullet exploded in front of him. He dropped to his knees and another bullet bit into the ground in front of him, spraying his face with dirt and sand. He clasped his hands to his face. For a moment he just sat there, rubbing sight back into his eyes.

The man at the windmill had a rifle trained on Clyde Shupe. The man in the tent had scrambled out and was gripping a rifle at waist level, pointing it toward the rest of us.

Clyde's face was purple with anger and insult. His chest heaved up and down. Suddenly he pushed himself to his feet and charged to his pickup. He staggered out with a rifle, but Milton Whetten and Sam Turley wrenched the gun from him. Clyde charged toward them and Preston Call and Clarence

Taylor grabbed him from behind and threw him up against the truck, pinning him there.

"Don't lose your head, boy," Grandpa commanded evenly, stepping over. "All you'll do is get somebody shot. And I'm not volunteering."

"That's our land!" Clyde wheezed. "They're not going to push us off our own land."

"That little patch of dirt isn't worth getting yourself killed over."

"I have a right to fight for what's mine."

"But you don't have the right to get the rest of us shot in the process," Grandpa snapped back. "We know one thing for sure. They mean business. They're not out here on a picnic."

"And so we let them have what they want?" Clyde called out.

Grandpa stared at him. Slowly he shook his head. "No, you don't lose everything, Clyde. Today you get to walk away — with your life."

"The trouble is, Jake," Calvin muttered, "it's not going to end with that little patch of ground."

"Calvin," Grandpa said, "right now those squatters don't have a thing to lose. If we did manage to throw them out today, what's going to stop them from sneaking back tomorrow? Or next week? Or some other time? But if we make the wrong move today, if somebody gets killed out here, we might lose the whole valley. We might end up fighting more than a handful of squatters."

"You should have done something," I said on our way back to Juarez. "Clyde Shupe needed help and everybody just stood around with their hands in their pockets."

"There was a time when I might have followed Clyde Shupe into that camp."

"Those people couldn't have shot us. They couldn't get away with something like that."

"What difference does it make if they do or don't get away with it if you're the one lying face down back there with your insides shot out? I had a brother who was shot down in circumstances not a whole lot different from what we faced this morning. And he happened to be in the right. His dispute was over a cow. But I would guess that if he was able to choose right now between that cow — or a hundred cows like it — he'd rather be alive."

# Chapter Five

That evening after dinner I sat in the living room. Grandpa was meeting with the men from Juarez at Calvin Cramer's place. Grandma had finished the dishes and come in to work on an afghan she was knitting.

I had been unable to get the incident at the agrarian camp out of my mind. The whole thing was unbelievable. It seemed bizarre that I had been so close to something so potentially violent. We had been shot at. There were men out there who were stealing land. Only forty-eight hours earlier I had been in a neat, orderly Arizona city where life was predictable. It was as though I'd stepped back in time when I had crossed the border at Palomas.

For several minutes Grandma worked quietly on her afghan. Then she looked up and asked, "What happened this morning?"

"Oh, nothing much," I mumbled uneasily. I reached for the *Reader's Digest* on the coffee table in front of me.

Grandma's hands worked swiftly, methodically. Her eyes stayed on me. "Did your Grandpa tell you to keep your mouth zipped?" she questioned.

I looked up. Grandma was smiling at me. Her dark eyes teased. She glanced down at her work and then up at me. "If nothing had happened out there this morning, your grandpa wouldn't be so tight-lipped. What happened?" she pressed.

41

"Nothing — much." She looked over at me, trying to appear stern but failing. "Really." I grinned. "Grandpa talked to them for a while. They didn't want to leave so . . . " I paused. "So we left. I mean, it was pretty simple."

"So why is everybody so tight-lipped?"

"Nothing to tell, I guess."

"You're not leaving anything out?"

"What's there to leave out?"

"It's plain to see that you're related to your grandpa," Grandma muttered. She studied me a moment. "I always thought you were like your grandpa. When you were just a little fellow, you'd follow him around and mimic his every move. You were quiet like he was. And stubborn. Being away from Colonia Juarez hasn't changed you much."

"Grandma," I asked, suddenly curious, "does Grandpa say much about his brother Harold?"

"What brings Harold up?"

"Tell me about him, about what happened to him. I've heard some, but . . . "

She was about to speak, then reconsidered. A mischievous smile pulled at the corners of her mouth. "Oh, Jacob, I don't know if a boy as young as you is ready for anything like that. I just don't know whether your youthful constitution could handle anything quite so — "

"Grandma," I broke in, only to have Grandma interrupt me again.

"Of course, you don't want to go around frightening old women with all kinds of wild tales. I feel the same way about frightening young boys."

"Nothing happened. You'd be disappointed."

"Try me."

"It was like I said, a lot of talk. I didn't even understand most of it. And then Clyde Shupe figured we ought to throw the bunch of them out right then and there."

"And."

I shrugged. "He started ripping down one of the tents."

42

"And."

I shrugged again. "Somebody took a potshot at him, and he ran for his gun to—"

"There were guns?"

"They missed. They were just trying to scare him."

"Where were the rest of you?"

"We were there. But no one got hurt or—"

"Marvelous."

"It was no big deal. I mean—"

"What would I have told your mother if you had—"

"Grandma, I was in the truck the whole time. Grandpa didn't even let me out. I felt like a two-year-old kid. Grandpa was the one who was right out in front of them. He was the one that could have been . . . " I stopped short.

"And nothing happened," Grandma stated. The familiar smile was gone now.

"It isn't as bad as you make it sound."

"As *I* make it sound?"

"Remember, Grandpa doesn't know I've told you any of this. What about Harold?"

With her jaw clamped tight, Grandma returned to her knitting, her hands moving rapidly. I watched her for a moment, wishing I had kept my mouth shut. I would know better the next time. "So that's why your Grandpa brought up Harold? Because nothing happened today."

"You said you'd tell."

For a long while Grandma worked without speaking. Finally she spoke. "Jake doesn't talk about it much. He never has. Your grandpa has been through a lot in his life, as much as half a dozen other men combined. More than once he thought he had lost his land. He had to start from scratch several times. Our oldest son, Clinton, died when he was two. Your Uncle Travis almost lost his life in a cattle stampede. For several days we wondered if he was ever going to pull out of it. He had been with your grandpa, so Jake thought it was his fault. But none of those things were as traumatic as when your grandpa and Harold were shot. It took a lot of years to erase the memories. For a good part of his life, he was terribly bitter. I didn't know how bitter until later. The men who shot and killed Harold were never brought to trial."

"Never?"

"Just one of the quirks of Mexican justice. A man might steal a loaf of bread and spend a year in jail. Somebody else might shoot a man and never even be arrested. It's just something that happens down here. It's hard to explain, especially to a young man who has just watched his older brother murdered."

"Did Grandpa ever . . . " I hesitated. "Did he ever try to even the score?"

Grandma looked up and stared across the room, not really seeing anything. "Like I said, your grandfather was a bitter man. At first it was something he kept locked inside him. For the first few years we were married I wasn't even aware that he felt so strongly. I knew the incident had happened, but I didn't realize it had been eating on him. And then it began to fester. And he couldn't keep it hidden. It was hard for both of us because—"

The front door opened and Grandpa walked in. Grandma returned to her afghan, and I began leafing through the *Reader's Digest*. Grandpa walked into the living room, dropped onto the sofa next to Grandma, and announced, "I'll be going to Chihuahua in the morning."

"Is that what you all decided?" Grandma asked.

Grandpa leaned his head back and rubbed his eyes with the balls of his hands. "There are still those that want to chase them off."

"Calvin Cramer?"

Grandpa nodded.

"Does Calvin own much land?" I asked. "I mean, does he have to worry more than anyone else?"

"He's got more land than most. He's done well for himself. But I think more than anything he's just spoiling for a fight.

He doesn't like to see any of the Mexicans push anybody from the colonies around."

"Do you think going to Chihuahua will do any good?" Grandma asked, without looking up from her work.

"I don't know. It's worth a try."

Grandpa yawned. "Do you think you could irrigate one of the orchards tomorrow?" he asked me. "The ditches are set. All you have to do is turn the pump on and let it run for a couple of hours and make sure it doesn't wash. If you think you can handle it, I'll leave it with you."

I would have preferred to go to Chihuahua with Grandpa, but I nodded and answered, "Sure, I can handle it."

"Would you like to call your mother tonight?" Grandma asked suddenly, changing the subject.

The question took me by surprise. The activity of the last twenty-four hours had made me forget everything from home. I smiled. "I've only been here a day, Grandma. I made it twenty-two months in Brazil without making a phone call home. I think I can make it here for a summer."

"Your folks will be anxious to know that you made it here all right."

"Oh, I don't know," I said with a smile, which was an attempt to disguise my true feelings. Both Grandpa and Grandma looked at me. I continued to thumb through the *Reader's Digest*. The pages were a blur.

"Jacob," Grandma spoke, "I don't know everything that's gone on between your mother and father. I haven't asked or tried to pry. I won't. But believe me, they want to know how you're doing."

"Do they?"

"Jacob, we know this is hard for you. But your parents need you, probably now more than ever."

"They've got a strange way of showing it."

I returned to my magazine, but after scanning the same paragraph a dozen times without really reading it, I realized concentration was impossible. I tossed the magazine to the coffee table and stood up. "I think I'll go to bed." I started for the door and stopped. Without looking back at either Grandma or Grandpa I spoke. "I'm sorry." I shrugged and looked at the floor. "There are some things I can't talk about. Not just now. Maybe in a while I'll feel like saying more."

In my room I undressed and then sat on the edge of my bed and thought of Mom standing in the lonely parking lot at the immigration office watching Grandpa and me drive away. A grim guilt nagged at my conscience. I wished then that I could go back and change that farewell. Mom deserved better. I knew that. Maybe Dad didn't, but Mom did, and that made me resent Dad even more. I was torn between love and pity for Mom and hate and anger for Dad. In the end I finally grabbed a pad and pen and wrote a quick note to Mom, telling her that I'd arrived safely and that everything was going fine. I managed to apologize for my cool behavior at the border. I expressed my love and appreciation. I stuffed the note into an envelope. But for some reason I never did send it.

# Chapter Six

The next morning I awoke to an empty, quiet house. I rolled over and stared sleepy-eyed at the alarm clock on the dresser. It was 7:15 A.M. I wondered why someone hadn't awakened me earlier. Then I remembered that Grandpa had gone to Chihuahua. I sat up, stretched, and padded down the hall to the bathroom where I showered and shaved before making my way to the kitchen.

A single place was set at the end of the table with a note propped up between the glass and the plate: "Jacob, I decided to go to Chihuahua with your grandpa. Scramble some eggs for breakfast and warm up the stew for lunch. We'll be back before five or six o'clock."

I whipped out a quick breakfast and then left the house for the orchard Grandpa had asked me to irrigate.

It was one of those quiet, peaceful mornings that are so rare outside places like Colonia Juarez. The morning sun was heating up, but the air was clean and fresh, filled with the noises of work and activity. On the way to the orchard I passed a crew of Mexican men chopping weeds along a ditch bank. Further on I spotted Mary Whetten's maid hanging out the morning wash. From somewhere down by the river a radio blared out mournful mariachi music. The atmosphere was reminiscent of so many places in Brazil where I had worked, and I was suddenly homesick for that faraway place that had become a second home for me. I longed to escape there, where life had been so innocent and charged with hope.

I breathed deeply as I wandered through the orchard. The trees were decked with thousands of small green apples that made the branches sag. I swished carelessly through the thick grass and clover and made my way to the diesel pump at the top of the orchard. After turning the pump on, I watched the icy crystal water pour from the eight-inch pipe and splash down the ditch toward the trees.

With my shovel over my shoulder, I wandered down through the orchard to the road, listening to the splash of water and the rumble of the diesel engine. It felt good to be there.

With a couple of hours to kill I headed leisurely back for the house. Just as I was leaving the orchard a white Ford LTD roared past me down the dirt street, leaving me choking in a cloud of dust. I covered my face with my hand, coughed and gasped for some clean air.

"What a maniac!" I muttered. As I turned down the street to Grandpa's place a few minutes later I spotted the same LTD pulled off the road and a girl in blue jeans and a flannel shirt bent over studying the car's front tire, which was flat.

"I guess that's what it takes to slow some people down," I remarked as I strolled by.

The girl straightened up and turned around.

"I hope you've got a spare," I grinned.

The girl didn't speak. She was about my age, maybe a little younger. Her hair was short with a bit of curl to it, all natural. She had a small mouth and a slightly upturned nose sprinkled lightly with freckles that were disguised by an olive tan.

"You almost ran me over back there," I said, stopping and nodding back toward the orchard.

"Maybe you ought to get off the roads."

"Let me know when you're out and about and I will."

She glared at me a moment and then turned and stomped back to the trunk, where she banged around in search of a jack. I was tempted to leave her to her misery, but I set my shovel down and ambled over to the back of the car.

"Need some help?" I offered.

"I can manage."

"If you change a tire like you drive, you should probably get some help."

She stopped her search and straightened up. At first glance she wasn't a grabbing beauty, but she was appealing. She had greenish-blue eyes that seemed to change to an intriguing shade of blue when the light shone just right. Or when she turned her anger on.

"I drive just fine. And I don't need any help changing a tire."

She returned to rummaging through the trunk, located the jack, and began tugging furiously on it.

"You might try removing that bolt first. If you don't, you'll probably tear out the whole rear end of your car before you get that jack loose." She glowered at me again. I raised my hands in surrender. "But I don't know anything. You've probably got a better idea."

She unscrewed the bolt, removed it, and then jerked the jack out and dropped it onto the ground. Reaching for the spare tire, she muttered, "Don't you have something better to do than stand around and watch me change my tire?"

"I can't think of anything right off. Not anything quite so entertaining."

She yanked the spare from the trunk, let it drop from the car onto the ground where it bounced and toppled onto her foot. Wincing, she bent over and grabbed her foot and turned her back to me.

"My offer still stands."

"I don't need your help."

I shrugged, bent over, grabbed the jack, and started for the front of the car.

"I said I didn't need your help."

"I know what you said, but at the rate you're going, it will be next week before you even figure out how this jack works."

"Who are you anyway?" she demanded, as I began jacking up the car.

"Jamison. Jacob Jamison."

The girl's mouth dropped open. "You're not little Jake, are you?"

I glanced up and shrugged. Nobody in my own family called me Jake. There was only one Jake—Grandpa. I was always Jacob, even around my friends. "Most people just call me Jacob."

"Oh. I'd heard you were coming. But . . . " She started to blush. "Did I really almost run you over?"

"I managed to get off the road. I almost suffocated in your dust, though."

"I'm sorry. I thought you were Chet Cramer. He deserves that every now and again."

"I haven't seen Chet around."

"You don't remember me, do you?"

I looked up and studied the girl. Her face wasn't a bit familiar. I shook my head. "Can't say that I do."

"Laurie Wagner."

My eyes narrowed as I stared. "Not little skinny Laurie Wagner with the freckles? The one with the mean left jab? You bloodied my nose during my first Twenty-fourth of July celebration in Colonia Juarez."

"The freckles have faded some. I wish I was still skinny. But I'm the same Laurie."

I shook my head. "Oh, I don't know about that. You've changed." I studied her as she smiled at me, displaying a set of straight white teeth. "I should have known that Laurie Wagner would be the only girl in Colonia Juarez driving like a—"

"All right," she cautioned, holding up her hands. "You've hounded me enough about my driving. I was just in a hurry. That back there wasn't anything personal. I didn't even know who you were."

"Are you still a tomboy, still the town bully?"

She shrugged and laughed. "Oh, maybe I've given up some of that."

"Little Laurie Wagner," I mused. "Who would have thought you would have . . . " I smiled and shrugged. "You look different. If I had known who you were, I wouldn't have been such a smart-mouth to you. I'm not out looking for any more fights. At least not after that one on Pioneer Day. And you picked that one. Over a lousy balloon."

Laurie laughed and bit down on her lower lip. "You were all right, Jake. A bit of a boob, but all right."

The two of us stared at each other for a moment and then I nodded toward the flat tire. "I don't know where you were headed, but you're never going to get there unless you get this tire changed."

"I was on my way to Casas. To get some parts for Dad's water pump. And now I guess I better pick up a new tire. Do you want to come?"

"Does that mean I have to change the tire?"

"I'm not giving you a ride to Casas for free."

"Do you make it a habit of picking up strangers?"

"Down here a girl can't be too fussy."

"That doesn't say much for me. Of course, you never were one to flatter a guy. Am I the best you've found so far?"

She grinned deviously. "You're the *only* thing I've found so far. And when I passed you back there, you didn't look like much from the back."

"And now that you've seen me from the front?"

"I'll tell you after you've changed my tire."

A few minutes later I was putting the jack away.

"Are you coming?"

"Can we make it back in a couple of hours? I've got to shut Grandpa's water off."

"Sure. The way I drive, we can be back in thirty minutes."

"The way you drive, I'll be pulling you out of a ditch before we make it halfway to Casas. But I'll come."

"What have you been doing with yourself the last few years?" Laurie asked as the wind gushed in from the window, whipping her hair and making her squint against the onslaught. She was becoming prettier all the time. She cocked her head as she glanced over at me, and the traces of a dimple appeared in her cheek.

"The usual, I guess." I slid down in my seat and hung my head toward the window so the warm morning air could rush in on me.

"I would have never picked you out in a crowd," Laurie admitted as the car challenged the steep dugway road leading up out of Colonia Juarez and toward Casas. "I do see the resemblance now."

"Well, that makes me feel better. I was hoping that I had changed some since you bloodied my nose. I wasn't much to look at back then."

"Who said you're much to look at now?" Laurie responded casually. "But I do need somebody to help me lug the pump parts." I glanced over at her. For a moment her face was a mask of stony indifference, and then it cracked into a teasing grin and she began to laugh.

"You're just full of compliments," I answered. "Why don't you let me off out here and I'll walk back?"

"Not on your life," she said, shaking her head. "If you think it's hard to pick up a guy in downtown Colonia Juarez, you ought to try out here in the middle of nowhere. Impossible!"

We both laughed. It felt good.

"Can we change the subject?" Laurie asked.

"Depends on what you change it to."

"To you," she answered with a shrug. "Did you ever try out for the basketball team like you bragged you were going to do?" She laughed. "You always talked like you were going to make it to the pros and join the Boston Celtics."

I chuckled. "Well, I gave up on all that."

"Why?"

"Got cut as a freshman."

"You're kidding," Laurie responded, suddenly serious. "I didn't mean to sound—"

I shook my head. "It's no big deal. I stopped mourning about it a long time ago. I don't even think about basketball much these days. I took up wrestling instead."

"You, a wrestler?"

"I did all right, if you don't mind me still bragging."

Laurie shuddered and shook her head in an obvious cringe. "Yuck! You mean you roll around on the floor with all those sweaty bodies? Doesn't it make you sick?"

"You get used to it. When you're fighting for your life, you don't think much about the other guy's sweaty armpit."

"Gag! Do you really like it?"

"I haven't made the pros, but," I added with a little pride, "I did manage to take state my senior year. That's more than I could have done bouncing an old ball up and down the court. At least with wrestling you can make it on your own. You can make it all the way to the top without worrying about dragging a whole team behind you."

"That's too bad."

"Why's that?"

"I guess I can't bloody your nose anymore when you need it."

"Why do you think I took it up? Just so tough girls like you couldn't push me around. I didn't mind the first time— until I found out you were a year younger than me."

"How are your mom and dad and sisters?"

The question was so sudden, so unexpected, like a slap in the face. I turned away and stared out the window. "They're still in Mesa," I answered, the easy humor of the moment gone.

"Well, I figured as much," Laurie laughed. "But how are they?" I didn't answer immediately, so she went on. "Is your dad still with the fire department?" She laughed again. "I can remember how you used to brag on him. It wasn't until I went to Mesa a few years ago that I discovered the city of Mesa had more than one fireman. The way you talked, I was sure your dad was a one-man fire department for the whole city. I was really quite disappointed. I liked your version better."

"He's still with the fire department," I muttered. "At least he was the last I heard."

Laurie glanced over at me. She studied me for a moment and saw the change. "Did I say something wrong, Jake?"

I pressed my lips together and shook my head without looking at her.

"I didn't mean to say anything wrong, Jake. Is your dad all right?"

I heaved a sigh. "Mom and Dad," I groped for words, "shall I say, are not compatible anymore."

"You mean, they've . . . broken up?"

"No, but I suppose that's always a possibility."

"I'm sorry. I didn't know."

"Not many do," I muttered. The last time I was in Mexico, I had come with the whole family. We were the perfect family then. I remembered how we walked to church together, all six of us. One of the older women in the Juarez ward had watched us stroll up the walk and commented that we looked just like an eternal family walking up the celestial road. I burned inwardly. What a contrast we were from that family eight years ago! Oh, we were still on the road. Just going in the opposite direction.

For the next few minutes we drove in silence, a blanket of depression thrown over our once jovial spirits. Every time I thought of Mom and Dad that same dismal depression descended and made me clam up.

"What have you been doing the last few years?" Laurie asked gently.

"Oh, the usual. I graduated from Mesa High a few years back and worked nine months in Mesa doing construction work. Then I left on my mission to Brazil. I got back three weeks ago."

"You're fresh out of the field then. Still jittery around girls and looking around for your companion. Now I understand why you've been clinging to the door handle."

I smiled. "I didn't know it was so obvious. I can slide over if you'd like."

"Oh, that's all right." She wagged a finger at me. "I like you shy. How long are you going to stay?"

"I've been thinking of staying the summer. And then going to BYU in the fall."

"I just got back from BYU the first of May," she said. "I already miss it. I'm beginning to wonder why I didn't stay for summer school."

"Why's that?"

She shrugged. "Not much going on down this way." She smiled. "But I guess I like it here. It's quiet and peaceful. It will make me appreciate going to school more. Are you going to be working for Jake?"

I nodded.

"Unless Jake has changed, he's pretty tight when it comes to money. Can't you make better money in Mesa doing construction?"

I chuckled. "I suppose I could make more money in Mesa. I didn't feel like I could stay there, though. And I didn't know where else to go. Not right now. I was able to save up quite a bit before my mission, and Mom and Dad wanted to pay for my mission. So I'm set as far as school is concerned. I guess I needed the peace and quiet of Colonia Juarez too."

"I'm sorry about your folks."

I nodded and then shrugged. "I guess I just haven't had time to adjust to the reality of it all." I stared straight ahead. "I came home from Brazil ready to take on the whole world. I had life by the tail. And then everything blew up in my face. That's why I'm here. I thought I might be able to sort things out down here where I don't always have the disaster staring me in the face."

For the next several minutes we were silent, speeding toward Casas in our own private worlds.

"Is there anything you'd like to see in Casas?" Laurie asked, breaking the silence and changing the subject.

"Ever since driving through with Grandpa the other day," I answered, "I've been dying to have one of those *paletas* they sell over at the little shop by the plaza."

"Great," she called out. "As soon as we pick up Dad's things, we'll drop over and pick up half a dozen. Or more." She grinned over at me.

By the time I reached Casas and became caught up in the hustle and confusion of the city's streets and shops and Laurie's company, Mom and Dad and home were locked away in the back of my mind.

We picked up the parts for the pump and then made a quick tour of Nuevo Casas Grandes. The narrow sidewalks were crowded with people, most of them women packing bags and bundles, pushing their way through the masses and into shops. Street vendors were everywhere selling everything from comic books to pots and pans. Many of them had their wares spread out on the narrow sidewalks for passersby to examine.

As Laurie and I strolled down the street, flowing with the crowds, curious dark eyes turned our way as though we were some novelty from a sideshow attraction. Young boys chased after us trying to sell us chewing gum and candy, and occasionally an older man would call out and offer us a watch, a pocketknife, or a lighter *"muy barato."*

We wandered over to the plaza and sat on a cement park bench.

"Has Casas changed much?" Laurie asked me.

"It's hard to tell. I don't know if things are different or if it's me." I shrugged. "Whatever it is, I like it. I've always liked Mexico. It's like stepping into another world, another time. Brazil was like that. The world out there in the States keeps rushing on, but down here you don't have to care."

"You make it sound like we're almost primitive here. We

do have television and radio, you know. We get El Paso stations. You can stay caught up with world news if you want to."

I shook my head. "That's just it. I don't want to. Grandpa and Grandma rarely flip on the TV. I like it that way."

"You hungry?"

"I'm always hungry."

"There's a little place that sells pizza on the other side of the tracks. They even use real mozzarella cheese. That's probably nothing to you, but down here that's innovation. It's not like going to the Pizza Hut in Mesa, but it's all right in a pinch."

"I've never been known to turn down a pizza, with or without mozzarella cheese."

We found the little pizza place, situated on a busy corner. It was painted a gaggy green, which seemed typical in Casas where buildings and homes were painted bright shocking colors. We pulled open the screen door of the pizza shop and stepped inside. Several fans turned lazily overhead and a portable fan was perched on the counter, breathing a bit of cool into the warm quarters. The floor was waxed. The dining area was crammed with small wooden tables that were draped with bright gingham tablecloths.

We found a corner table where we could look out the front window and watch the street. A man took our order and yelled it back to the kitchen. For a moment we were quiet, content to be silent, hidden observers.

"When I was younger," I finally spoke, "I wanted to come to Mexico and live with Grandpa. Mexico was so — " I shrugged. "Fascinating. Intriguing. I was always envious of the rest of you who had Mexico all to yourselves."

Laurie smiled at me across the table. "And I was always envious of people like you who could live in the States and eat all the Big Macs, french fries, and mozzarella cheese you wanted."

"Are you still envious?"

"Sometimes. But I like Mexico. The older I get the better

I understand that there's more to life than Big Macs and french fries."

"Do you ever think of leaving Mexico? Not just to go to BYU. I mean leave for good."

Laurie pondered a moment. "I'm torn, I suppose. I want to graduate from BYU in interior design. I'd like to come back here after that, but what does a person with a degree in interior design do in a place like Colonia Juarez?"

"You could design one heck of a living room," I laughed.

"And I'd like to do that. I'm not dying to have a career for the rest of my life, but I'd like to try it for a while. That leaves Colonia Juarez out. Besides, by the time I'm finished with college I'm not sure there will be much to come back to."

"How do you mean?"

She shrugged. "I guess we're just running out of room. Everybody down here either ranches or runs an orchard, and there are only so many of them to go around. That means only a few of us growing up down here will be able to stay. The rest will have to leave. If I were to stay, I'd have to marry someone from down here."

"And you don't want to do that?"

"I don't think so. At least, right now I can't think of anyone that would interest me."

"And if there was?"

Laurie smiled and stared out into the street at an old man hobbling across the intersection. He was completely oblivious to the blaring horns, screeching brakes, and angry shouts he was causing. "Even then I'm not sure. Things are so different now. Mexico has changed drastically since you were here. If it changes that much in the next eight years, maybe none of us will be here. Colonia Juarez will be just a memory."

"You sound like Grandpa."

Laurie looked down at the table and wrote on the gingham cloth with her finger. "Sometimes things seem the same. Other times I feel as though we're just waiting for everything to blow up in our faces. Like when we pass the Paquimé and I see all

the state police with their guns and their angry faces. And I
see the people in the shops with their pockets full of worthless
money and wonder how much longer they can go on like that.
And then there are the agrarians who are moving onto our
land. I get scared and wonder how much longer we'll be able
to keep on like we have. Is everything going to just tumble
down around us?"

"The world can tumble down around you living in the
States, too," I remarked seriously.

Laurie looked across the table at me. "I'm sorry about your
folks," she whispered.

"Some things just happen, I guess. Down here the economy falls apart. Out there — well, out there other things fall
apart."

"Is everything over between them?"

I thought for a moment. I pressed my lips together and
then answered, "It's hard to say. Right now it doesn't look
good. I can't help but hope that they'll work things out. It
makes me angry, though. You know, them messing things up
so bad. But I really think the storm will pass and we'll all get
back together. I'm not sure it will ever be the same, but — "

"There are probably happier things we can talk about,"
Laurie suddenly said, beginning to smile. Just then a huge
Mexican lady, wearing a soiled apron, navigated her way among
the tables and chairs in the dining area and brought us a steaming pizza. She set it down, said something to Laurie in Spanish,
and then returned to the kitchen area.

"You speak like a native," I remarked.

"Everybody does down here. You have to. You go to school
in the morning and everything is in English. You go back in
the afternoon and everything is in Spanish. Everybody that
graduates from the academy is bilingual." She bit into her
wedge of pizza and then warned, "Watch out for the green
chili. This is pizza with a Mexican twist."

I ignored her warning and took a huge bite. It was good,
but it was hot! Hot enough to make my eyes water and my

nose run. I had to wash down each bite with lemonade just to keep my mouth cooled off.

"Tell me about the future Boston Celtic that gave up basketball for wrestling," Laurie asked, sipping her drink.

I smiled and shrugged. "You know how you dream that you're going to do something. That one thing can be your whole life. You sleep and breathe it. Your whole reason for doing so many things all goes back to that one goal. When you have time to yourself, that's what you think about. Have you ever felt like that?"

"I wanted to be a gymnast."

"You?"

"And what may I ask is wrong with that?"

"I'm sorry," I apologized, ducking my head. "You just didn't seem the type. I mean back then. You were always so rough and tumble. I'd pick you for girl athlete of the year or something but—"

"But not a gymnast?"

I shrugged. "I guess not."

"Well, that's what I wanted. Maybe my rough-and-tumble ways were just a cover-up for a dream I had to postpone. I cut out pictures. I loved the Olympics, Nadia Comaneci and the others. I even bought books and tried to teach myself."

"What made you change your mind?"

"One day I was trying to decide when I could really begin my training. I knew I needed lessons or something. You had to have a coach. Anybody that did anything in gymnastics had a coach. In my dreams I had always imagined somebody from Juarez marrying a girl from the States who would come down here and teach me." She pushed her pizza back and stared down at the table. "But that morning—I still remember it well—I was out in our backyard doing handstands and cartwheels." She shrugged. "I suddenly realized I was chasing a dream that would never be. No one was ever coming to teach me. And by the time I was old enough to go to the States and find my own trainer, I would be too old to be a gymnast. I cried. It was hard letting go of something I'd carried around with me so long, something that had given me something to shoot for."

I leaned back in my chair and stared across the table at Laurie. "Then I guess you know how I felt about the Boston Celtics," I said softly. "It didn't take a genius to tell me I didn't have the height, the speed, or the skill to ever make it to the pros. What was a real shock was to discover I didn't even have what it took to make it on the high school freshman team. I had to pack a lot of dreams away that day. And when they were gone, I felt like a stranger in an empty house."

"So what happened?"

"Three days later the wrestling coach asked me to try out for the team. He said I was built like a wrestler. So I redecorated my house with different dreams. I haven't looked back since. I guess the real key is that once you've chased a dream down a dead-end road, you start looking for another dream."

We were quiet for a moment and then I remarked, "Aren't we a fine pair of philosophers? It must be the green chili. I don't ever get this way at Pizza Hut. I just stuff my face and don't think at all."

"Why, the two of us could solve the world's problems if we had enough time and enough pizza. With green chili."

I laughed. "Let's head over to the bakery. I want to buy one of those molasses pigs Grandma used to bring home to me."

As we left the pizza shop and headed across the street to the *panadería*, the Mexican bakery, a bus came roaring around the corner and almost ran us down. I grabbed Laurie's hand and pulled her back just as the bus rumbled past. For a moment we stood there, a little shaken, still holding hands. We checked the traffic again and then proceeded, hand in hand. On the other side of the street I was about to loosen my grip on Laurie's hand, but it felt comfortable there. She had a small hand, soft, smooth and warm. I tightened my grip. "Crazy bus," I muttered in an attempt to cover my bold move.

Laurie laughed and squeezed my hand. "I'm kind of glad that old bus came along." She hugged my arm and I blushed, but I knew she was feeling the same thing I was.

"It's been a while since I took a girl's hand to do anything but shake it." I blushed slightly.

"You getting nervous? I can walk at arm's length if you'd like."

"I'm adjusting all right," I said, grinning.

It was late afternoon when Laurie finally dropped me off at Grandpa's place. We had been all over Casas. We had sucked icy *paletas*, sipped cool lemonade, strolled around the plaza, and talked. Mostly we had just laughed and talked and discovered that not all friendships fade with time.

"It's been fun," Laurie remarked, smiling over at me as I opened the car door to step out. "Thanks for helping me with Dad's things."

She was pretty. I wondered why I hadn't seen it immediately. All day I'd watched her become prettier. "Anytime you need some help you know where to find me," I said.

"Now don't go hide yourself away someplace where no one can find you."

"Don't worry. I've got a premonition that some evening I'm going to get this terrible craving for some deep philosophizing and Mexican pizza. And you're the only person I know who can show me the way."

"You're back," I greeted Grandma and Grandpa as I stepped into the kitchen. Their conversation stopped immediately, and Grandma pushed herself to her feet and smiled broadly. Grandpa stayed at the table, somewhat somber. "Did you get along all right?" Grandma called to me. Her smile disappeared momentarily and she scolded, "You didn't touch the stew. All you had to do was warm it up. What did you do for lunch?"

I stepped to the sink and grabbed a glass from the cupboard. "Pizza."

"Pizza? Where did you get pizza around here?"

"Laurie Wagner picked me up and took me to Casas."

"Did you get along all right with the orchard?" Grandpa asked.

I froze, staring down into the sink. Then I whipped around and stared at Grandpa. "I forgot," I muttered.

He shook his head indifferently. "No problem. We'll get it tomorrow."

"But I turned the water on," I rasped, feeling sick. "I just forgot to turn it off."

"You mean it's still running? The place will be flooded."

I wasn't listening. Already I was rushing toward the door. I ran most of the way to the orchard. When I was still half a block away, I could see huge puddles in the road where the water had spilled over the ditch banks. I scrambled through the fence and sloshed my way up the hill through the soggy sod, surveying the results of my negligence. I trudged through the mud, patching gaping holes, digging new channels, and trying to put things back the way they had been.

The sun was beginning to set when I first noticed Grandpa. He had come quietly and started on the other side of the orchard and worked toward me. As dusk darkened into night and we drew closer together, I realized that I would have never finished without his help. It was my mistake, but Grandpa was there to pull me through.

"I'm sorry," I muttered when we finally met in the middle of the orchard. I was tired and covered with sweat and dried mud. "You should probably just give me a good hard kick in the rear and be done with it."

Grandpa banged his mud-caked shovel on a rock. "You figure that would take care of the orchard?" Grandpa asked.

"It might make you feel better."

He didn't answer. Together we started home. I wanted him to say something, criticize me, yell at me, anything but silence. When he did speak, his remark was completely unexpected. "I didn't know that the Wagner girl was—" He cleared his throat. "She must have grown up while I wasn't noticing. She was just a bean sprout the last time I bothered to look. What is she, fifteen or sixteen now?"

"She just finished her sophomore year at BYU," I muttered.

"Hmm, she has grown. It's going to be harder to keep you busy than I thought. I figured I'd get you down here away from all the distractions and I'd get loads of work out of you." He shook his head. "I guess Colonia Juarez has some mighty distracting things, too."

I felt my cheeks warm with embarrassment, and I was glad for the cover of darkness. "We just went down to get some parts for her dad," I explained lamely. "It was no big deal."

"And stayed all day? You must have got yourselves lost. I didn't know Casas was so big."

"She just showed me around a bit."

"When we went through two days ago, I showed you around a bit. But," he added dryly, "it didn't take us all day."

"Well," I stammered, "she showed me some places you didn't."

"Had I known about those places, I would have shown them to you two days ago and saved you a trip today. The orchard would have been better off, too."

"I'm sorry about the orchard."

Grandpa laughed, and I knew he wasn't angry.

"How did things go in Chihuahua City?" I asked.

Suddenly he was solemn. "We talked."

"Just talked?"

"At least nobody shot at us."

"So the trip was a waste?"

"I hope not. We had a good visit with Carlos Alvarez."

"Who's he?"

"An adviser to the governor. He's helped us out of other jams in the past. He understands our situation here. In fact, when he was younger he attended school at the academy. He's got his finger in a lot of pots, and the governor trusts him.

Potentially, he's one of the most powerful men in Chihuahua. We're lucky to have him on our side."

"What do you do now?"

"Wait. That's all we can do. That's also probably the hardest thing to do."

"So the agrarians stay?"

"For the time being."

"You can always try Calvin's way."

"I have a feeling that's what Calvin is going to say."

"Maybe Calvin's way is the best way," I remarked. "That's what I'd do if I were calling the shots."

"When a horse goes lame, you try a lot of different things before you go out and shoot it."

# Chapter Seven

My first Sunday morning in Colonia Juarez I slept late. It was 8:20 before I got up. I'd been here almost a week now. And I felt it. During the last two days I had ridden horseback with Grandpa, rounding up cattle south of Colonia Juarez and moving them upriver on the opposite side of town. Saddle sore took on new meaning. My hands had blistered and begun the makings of calluses. The back of my neck was sunburned and peeling. My shoulders and back were stiff and sore. Ironically, it all felt good. There was something rewarding about the throb of aching muscles. I groaned as I turned over in bed and stretched.

Since my blunder in the orchard, I had been promoted to partner instead of mere tagalong. Grandpa expected me to work and work hard. If a calf broke from the herd and bolted for the brush because I was too casual about my responsibilities, Grandpa wasn't above hollering at me and telling me to wake up. He hated complaining, laziness, and shoddy work, and he didn't hesitate to grumble at me if I was involved in any of the three. I would have resented those kinds of demands from anyone else, but coming from Grandpa, I understood, grumbled back, and loved it.

Grandpa wasn't a talker, but then neither was I. We could work together for an hour and exchange only a few words, but there was so much more communicated in our silence. Though he never said so, I was convinced he was glad I was there. But not as glad as I was. Working with Grandpa I didn't have a chance to worry about home. For the time being there was only one home—Colonia Juarez.

Occasionally Uncle Travis was with us, but he was on a different level. He was more businesslike than Grandpa and was tied up more with the management of the ranch and orchards. He handled the books, directed the hired help, made most of the trips to the bank, to Casas, to the Paquimé, and so forth. The ranch and the orchards were a business to him. His biggest concerns were efficiency and profits.

Grandpa disliked the books, the business side of the ranch. He preferred to be out getting his hands dirty, sweating under a burning sun or wielding a shovel. Financially, he was well enough off. Labor was cheap. He could have hired someone to do the hard work, but work was why he had the ranch and the orchards in the first place. Hard work was his love and life.

There was a soft tapping at my door. "Jacob," Grandma called to me in a whisper, "are you awake?"

I pushed myself up on my elbow and stared sleepily toward the door. "Yeah, I'm awake."

Grandma pushed the door open a crack and peeked in. "Your grandpa is going to church in San Diego. Would you like to drive out with him? It's a beautiful morning for a drive."

"San Diego?"

"You remember San Diego. The little place south of here, the one just south of Cuautemoch."

"Oh, there," I answered, remembering vaguely. "He was branch president there once, wasn't he?" Grandma nodded. "Does he want me to go?"

"He didn't really say," Grandma admitted. "But," she added quickly, a little embarrassed, "he usually doesn't ask. I know he would want you to go. He likes to take everyone to San Diego."

"Sure, I'll go with him."

68

Forty minutes later Grandpa and I were in the truck heading out of Colonia Juarez on a dirt road for San Diego. It was an awesome kind of morning. Sunday in Colonia Juarez was like that. It was as though some magician waved his wand over the valley and transformed it. On Sunday everything ground to a halt. Tractors and trucks sat idle, horses grazed contentedly, and shovels, saws, and hammers hung on tool shed walls.

As we bounced over the rough dirt road, Grandpa dodged the rocks and ruts and whistled softly to himself. He was happy, thoroughly content. I watched him from the corner of my eye and smiled. The rough, rugged gruffness so characteristic of him was gone, replaced with the simple smile, the high tilt of the head, and the spark in his gaze.

"You're happy today," I observed, grinning over at him.

He pulled the corners of his mouth down for a moment, then shrugged and allowed the smile to return. "Yeah, I suppose I am."

"What's the occasion?"

He took a deep breath and savored it. "It's Sunday," he explained simply. "No work."

I laughed. "I thought you lived for work."

"Oh, I suppose I do. I like to work until I'm beat, until I can't do another thing. And all the while I'm thinking how good it's going to feel when I can rest on Sunday." He laughed.

"You mean you work until it hurts because you know how good it's going to feel when you quit?"

"Something like that."

"What brings you to San Diego?" I asked. "Are you still branch president?"

"I guess they're putting me out to pasture."

"Are you anything out here? I mean, do you have a job or something?"

He shook his head and whistled softly.

"Then why do you even bother to come? What's there in San Diego?"

Grandpa smiled over at me and then gazed down the road. "It's home."

"San Diego? I thought Colonia Juarez was home."

"It is. But San Diego is —" He paused and pondered. "San Diego is a different kind of home. San Diego, well, is my own personal refuge."

I laughed. "I guess I don't remember what San Diego is like. I didn't think there was much there. It didn't ever seem like much of anything to me, just a spot in the road. Has it changed that much in the last eight years?"

Grandpa shook his head. "Probably not."

I began to laugh again. "What's so funny?" Grandpa asked.

I shrugged. "It seems strange that you got stuck out here in the boonies."

"Stuck out here in the boonies? How's that?"

"Oh, here you've worked in the Church all your life. You were stake president for years. You've been a stake missionary. You've been in bishoprics. And then when you get a little older, what happens to you? You end up in a third-rate village like San Diego. It seems unfair. You know, kinda like they've . . . " I searched for the right word.

"Like they put me out to pasture?"

I grinned. "Well, I wasn't going to say it just like that." I paused, then asked. "You don't feel any of that?"

For a minute Grandpa didn't answer. I thought he was going to ignore the question. Then he took a deep breath and said, "The time will come for each of us to stand before the Lord and explain what we've done with our life. There has to be some purpose to our existence. I've thought about that moment many times. Maybe more lately than before. I guess I'm beginning to finally realize that I don't have an indefinite lease on life."

"Ah, come on, Grandpa, you're going to live forever, and you know it. You're too ornery to just die."

He smiled. "Oh, it will come, all right." He pondered another moment. "And when that time comes and the Lord asks me to explain my existence, I'll show him my family. And then I'll show him San Diego. And I really don't think he'll ever ask me whether I spent a day of my life as stake president or anything else like that."

"What does San Diego have to do with anything?"

There was a far-off look in Grandpa's eyes as he stared down the road. "I baptized most of the people in San Diego," he remarked softly. "I was the one that introduced them to the Church. A few years ago San Diego had only a handful of members. Now it's one of the most active branches in the whole Juarez Stake. I was the first branch president there. They're my people, Jacob."

"I thought the people in Juarez were your people."

He nodded. "But they came naturally. They were always mine. I had to work to make the people in San Diego mine. Maybe that's the difference."

"So San Diego is kind of like your mission field?"

"Yes, but more than just a mission field."

I was quiet, suddenly reflective. My mind wandered back to another time, another place—Boa Vista, a small town in northern Brazil. There was a thriving branch there now, but that hadn't always been. My most frustrating moments had been spent in Boa Vista. I had worked harder there. I had hated more there. And yet, when I thought back on my mission, Boa Vista epitomized my time in Brazil.

San Diego was a quiet, peaceful place that Sunday morning. Most of the village's thirty-five or forty homes were brown, sunbaked adobe. A few had been whitewashed. Others had been stuccoed and painted a bright blue or a glaring green. There were no paved streets, just a narrow dirt road. A few struggling trees and several small gardens were the only vegetation in the village.

San Diego couldn't be considered a pretty place, perhaps typically Mexican, but not pretty. It boasted no innate beauty, only a plain simplicity.

To the west of San Diego was part of Grandpa's range. To

the east and winding its lazy way through thick willows and giant cottonwood trees was a small meandering stream. Actually, it was more a trickle than a stream. East of the stream and just outside the village was a low sloping hill covered with grass and spotted with blackberry bushes at its summit. At the foot of the hill stood a modest building with a tin roof, open eaves, and pale blue framed windows. The house had been stuccoed and painted white. A white picket fence surrounded it with a double gate on the west side and two rosebushes growing at each gate post. Inside the fence was a struggling lawn, the only real lawn in all of San Diego. A gravel path led from the road, over a wooden footbridge that crossed the stream and wound its way to the gate, past the rosebushes, and eventually to the building's double doors.

In any other place this plain building would have gone unnoticed, but in San Diego it held a position of prominence. It was the first thing a person noticed when approaching the community.

"That's the *casa de oración*, the prayer house," Grandpa announced, pointing to this building, which had already caught my attention.

"You mean your chapel?"

Grandpa nodded. "Everybody calls it the *casa de oración*."

"It doesn't look like a regular church," I observed.

Grandpa shook his head. "It's not. I mean it's not a dedicated building. The people are hoping the Church will approve a regular chapel here. The prospects are looking better all the time. Until then, though, this will have to do."

I smiled. "I'm beginning to feel like I'm back in Brazil. Too bad the people don't speak Portuguese here. I'd eat it up."

Grandpa chuckled. "Oh, you'll be able to get by."

When we arrived, the chapel doors were open. As we climbed from the truck, crossed the bridge, and started up the gravel path, an older man, about Grandpa's age, dressed in dark pants and a white shirt without a tie, came to the doorway. His hair was thick, wavy, streaked with gray and combed back from his forehead. As soon as he spotted us, his face exploded into a wide smile. He waved and called over his shoulder to someone inside, *"Lupe, ya viene el hermano."*

A moment later a heavy woman, shorter than the man and only a year or two his junior, came to the door; her face lighted up with a smile and welcome sparkled from her dark eyes. *"Hermano!"* she called out, hurrying down the gravel path to where Grandpa and I stood. She rushed up to Grandpa, threw her arms about him in an affectionate Mexican *abrazo*. The man followed her, shook Grandpa's hand, and then gave an *abrazo* as well.

Grandpa turned to me and said, "This is José Luís Aragón and his wife, Guadalupe." The old couple pumped my hand vigorously, gave me an *abrazo*, and chattered a Spanish greeting that had a familiar ring to it. But what my ears couldn't decipher my heart understood. These people were geniune, completely without guile as the scripture would say. "José Luís works for Travis and me," Grandpa explained. "I couldn't ask for a better hand. He's also the first person I ever baptized from San Diego. Thirty-six years ago. Now he's the president of the branch here."

Soon the chapel yard was filled with people, scrubbed and dressed in their Sunday best. As each one arrived, he pushed his way toward Grandpa, clasped his hand in friendship, and pulled him close in a warm *abrazo*. By virtue of my relationship to Grandpa, I was treated to the same welcome. I felt like a new junior companion in my first city.

Because of the gathering that occurred around Grandpa and me, the meeting was fifteen or so minutes late in starting. When we finally did enter the *casa de oración*, I was intrigued. The chapel's interior was plain and simple but uniquely inviting. The building boasted one large meeting room and two small classrooms. The walls were all white; the rafters, bare and uncovered. The wooden floor was sanded smooth, but unfinished. There were eight rows of homemade wooden benches in the chapel area and a half dozen rows of folding chairs behind the benches. In front of the chapel area was a homemade podium. The sacrament table was little more than a wooden bench draped with white tablecloths, but it blended well in this rustic setting.

During the meetings, I understood very little of the Spanish, but I was content to be present as an observer. These people weren't here for show. They were here to feel of the Spirit. And there was a special spirit there, one I hadn't ever felt before outside of Brazil.

There was no piano, but its absence did little to daunt the members' musical enthusiasm. They sang out loud and strong, although a little off-key, but no one seemed to mind.

There was no clock on the wall. But these people weren't interested in a clock. No one was just putting in his weekly block of meeting time. These people wanted to be in that simple chapel with each other.

When the benediction was offered, there was no mad scramble for the front doors. Everyone lingered and visited, oblivious to Sunday dinner and afternoon naps.

"Well," Grandpa asked as we drove toward Colonia Juarez, "what did you think of San Diego?"

"It's kind of small. Not much to it really. I mean there's not much to look at. Definitely not one of Mexico's big tourist attractions. But," I pondered as we bounced along, "the people are hard to explain. They're happy, aren't they. They don't have much, but they don't seem to know that. That's the way people were in Brazil. I guess that's why I love Brazil so much, why I'd like to go back."

Grandpa began to whistle. I thought he was working on "The Day Dawn Is Breaking," but his pitch was so bad I couldn't tell for sure. I smiled, thinking I knew why the members in San Diego sang off-key.

"Where did the chapel come from?" I asked, anxious to talk.

Grandpa ruminated a moment. "In the beginning the members from San Diego met with the Mexican Ward in Colonia

74

Juarez. When there were enough members to hold meetings in San Diego, they met in José Luís's house. But after a year or so that was too small. I owned the land down by the creek, so one day I decided I'd build a little something that they could meet in. They weren't big enough for the Church to come in and build something. I didn't have anything elaborate in mind. Just four walls and a roof.

"José Luís and I worked in our spare time. At first it was a two-man project. But as the weeks passed, people dropped by for an hour or so to lend a hand. We poured the foundation and made our own adobe bricks. Gradually more and more people became involved. It wasn't long before members and nonmembers alike were lending a hand. It became a community project. It's still a community building. Soon we had people wanting to be baptized. We worked on the house for months because it was all volunteer labor. Before long we realized that with as many people as were being baptized our little house was going to be too small even before we finished it. So we changed our plans and made it larger.

"I don't remember now how long it took us to finish it. We were meeting in it as soon as there was a roof over our heads. Later we stuccoed the adobe walls." Grandpa smiled. "As the years passed, we made little improvements here and there. We painted it, put on a good roof, hung some good doors, and put in decent windows. Then when the house looked nice, we decided we would need to do something about the yard. That's when we put up the picket fence and planted the grass and flowers. It's a beautiful place now." He glanced over at me. "Maybe not beautiful in the same way chapels in Mesa, Arizona, are beautiful. I suppose from an architect's point of view our little prayer house is pretty crude, but when you see all the time, the labor and the love that's gone into that building, it's mighty beautiful."

"Is everybody in San Diego a Mormon now?" I asked.

"Maybe a few more than half."

"And the others aren't interested?"

"We're still working on them. We're patient. We'll get them all. When I started out, José Luís was the only one who joined the Church. Every Sunday he came to Colonia Juarez for meetings. It was almost five years before Lupe and their kids softened up and joined. It was a lot of years after that before anybody else took the plunge. In the beginning there was a little animosity, but that disappeared a long time ago. Now when there's a branch party, the whole village shows up. If somebody needs help, nobody asks if they are a member or not. Everyone pitches in and helps."

"You're a different person in San Diego," I observed.

Grandpa looked away and nodded. "Yes," he said softly, "I guess I am. I feel different." He smiled. "Sometimes life reaches out, grabs and shakes you, throws you to the ground. It's at times like those that I like to drive out to San Diego on a Sunday morning and get life back into focus." He glanced over at me.

"Is that why you brought me out here?" I asked. "Because you figure I need to put things back into focus?"

"I came for me. Jacob, everybody needs a San Diego."

I smiled. "Maybe I feel a little that way about Colonia Juarez." I became serious as I thought of home. "But for some people it will take more than a San Diego to put life back into focus. Sometimes," I mused under my breath, "life gets so messed up you can never get it back into focus."

# Chapter Eight

"So where have you been hiding yourself?" a voice called to me as I strolled into La Sorpresa, the small general store in Colonia Juarez, and let the metal frame screen door clatter behind me. I turned to see Laurie Wagner coming from the checkout stand with a bag of groceries. "I looked for you in church Sunday. Have you gone inactive?" she teased.

"I didn't know anyone was going to notice." I could feel my cheeks coloring as Laurie approached and smiled up at me. I'd been thinking of her ever since our trip to Casas.

"I haven't seen you around much," she said. It was an accusation but in fun.

"Oh, I've been around. In fact, I've been all over. I can hardly walk. Grandpa doesn't want me running off to town with any more strange women. The last time I tried that I got into kind of a jam. I flooded the orchard."

"And you had the nerve to tease me about my driving."

We both laughed.

"Hey, I've got to get moving," I injected quickly, backing down one of the aisles and bumping into a small Mexican woman with her arms loaded with groceries. I mumbled an embarrassed apology to her and then turned back to Laurie. "Grandma sent me up for some meat. This is what you do to me every time. Whenever you show up, I forget what I'm supposed to be doing and start bumping into people and messing everything up." Just then I accidentally brushed my elbow along the shelf, sending three cans of soup clattering to the floor and rolling down the aisle. I lunged after them, scooped them up, and returned them to the shelf, my cheeks burning.

"I guess I better let you go," Laurie said, trying not to giggle. She raked her hair with her fingers and shifted her package to her other arm. "If Jake doesn't have you working till midnight, why don't you drop by Spilsbury's arena this evening. They're going to be doing some roping there. It's a far cry from a ripsnortin' rodeo, but it's something to do on a Tuesday night."

"I'm not much of a roper," I remarked.

"You can watch, can't you?"

"Are you going to be there?" I asked.

She chewed on her tongue. "I thought I might drop by. To watch the roping, of course."

I nodded and smiled. "Maybe I'll try to make it." I grinned. "To watch the roping, of course."

I hurried through dinner and excused myself from the table. "Where you off to in such a hurry?" Grandma laughed, as I carried my plate and glass to the sink.

"Oh, I thought I'd run over to the arena for a few minutes. Some of the guys are going to be doing some roping."

"I can get you something to rope," Grandpa commented dryly from the table.

I shrugged. "I was planning on watching."

"Watching what? That little Wagner girl isn't going to show up, is she?"

"Wagner girl? Is she a roper?"

"She must be. She roped you." He began to chuckle and shake his head. "When she was in pigtails and overalls, I worried less about her. I think you did too."

"I know what to do around a girl," I grumbled.

Grandpa nodded. "That's what I'm afraid of." He stretched and groaned. "Maybe I'll drop over there myself."

"Are you going to rope or just keep an eye on me?"

He pushed his chair back. "I won't need to keep an eye on you if you keep your eyes on the ropers."

I left the house as casually as I could, taking my time as I strolled across the yard and jumped the chain-link fence. But once I crossed the bridge and took the path along the river underneath the cottonwood trees, I shifted into a high-geared walk.

Reaching the arena, I spotted Laurie right away. She stood next to the rail fence with two other girls. Several guys were nearby while a dozen younger kids were running around, pushing, shoving, and calling to one another.

Three men were at the chute, and a half dozen riders were in the arena, joking, galloping their horses, and testing their rope. There was a thin haze of dust hanging in the air. Occasionally a calf bawled.

A few feet from where Laurie and her friends stood, seven or eight Mexican men and boys sat perched on the top rail of the fence, watching the action inside the arena.

Everything was low-key. There was no rush or set order to things. I could tell right away that this was more a social gathering than a roping exhibition.

Laurie spotted me as soon as I walked up, and she broke away from the others and walked toward me. She was wearing a pair of Levi's, a cotton shirt, and a pair of white tennis shoes. Her hands were pushed into her pockets and there was a touch of blush on her cheeks as she sidled up to me and bumped against my shoulder.

"I wondered if you were going to show," she greeted me with a smile.

"I had to shut the water off." I grinned. "You've already got Grandpa on guard. He thinks there's something up," I added in a whisper. "He's even coming down in a while to check up on me."

Laurie cocked her head to one side. "I guess you'll have to behave yourself for a change then." She took my arm and squeezed it. "Come over and meet the others."

"You all remember Jacob Jamison, don't you?" Laurie introduced me as we strolled up to the group Laurie had just left. "He used to come down here all the time. He's Jake's grandson."

The talking stopped and all eyes turned on me. The two girls smiled. The guys glared. I fidgeted, suddenly uncomfortable and vulnerable.

"This is Cindy Brown and Valerie Johnson," Laurie began the introductions, nodding at the two girls. "That's Bill Romney," Laurie said, pointing to a blond boy astride the fence. "The one next to him is Randy Hatch. And these two," Laurie said, pointing toward two guys leaning against the pole fence, "are Tom Cluff and Benny Call. That's Bryan Turley," she said, motioning to a wiry redhead. "And," she added, "you remember Chet Cramer." She nodded toward a rider who had walked his bay horse to the fence and now sat leaning heavily on his saddle horn.

I looked up at Chet and our gazes locked momentarily. Chet was about my size and had a dark handsome face with greenish-blue eyes and thick black eyebrows. His black hair was full and curly and stuffed under a straw cowboy hat. I vaguely remembered the names of the others from previous visits, but I remembered Chet well, even though he looked different now. He and I had been pretty decent friends at one time. But just now I didn't get the impression the friendship had endured.

"Hello, Chet," I said, attempting a smile. Chet didn't say anything. He nodded once in my direction and then studied Laurie.

Feeling conspicuous in the middle of these strangers, I stepped over to the fence and looked inside as a rider spurred his mare and galloped after a calf that had just been forced from the roping chute. Laurie followed me to the fence.

"Is this a closed party?" I asked in a husky whisper. "Or is that the welcome they give everyone?"

Laurie laughed. "Oh, you just have to give them time to warm up."

Just then Chet Cramer said something in Spanish, and there was an explosion of laughter from the group. I turned to find all eyes on me. I looked away.

"Don't worry about them," Laurie whispered, touching my arm. "They don't mean anything."

"You planning to ride?" Chet Cramer asked, riding over to me. He dismounted and climbed over the fence, dropping down next to Laurie. Immediately I detected a challenge.

"I hadn't thought much about it," I answered.

"Done any roping?"

Over the years Grandpa had taught me to do a little roping. At least I knew some of the fundamentals. I had been able to throw a rope and lasso a post. I had even roped a few calves once or twice from horseback. Of course, that was eight years ago, but I wasn't about to admit that to Chet.

"I used to do a little roping with Grandpa," I grinned. "I have an uncle that owns a ranch in Arizona. I've done some roping there, too. But I'm a little out of practice. I haven't done much the last two or three years."

"If you ever had the knack," Chet commented, "you don't lose it."

"I had it."

Chet shrugged. "You ought to give it a try then."

"I came to watch."

"Usually the guys come to rope." He laughed. "The girls do the watching for us."

I stiffened. I wanted to say something in my defense, but before I could, Chet pushed away from the fence and rejoined the others.

I watched him walk away. "What's he all blown up about?" I asked, more to myself than to Laurie. "Does he play top dog with everybody that shows up down here?"

"That's just Chet," Laurie said, sighing.

I studied Chet and the others. Most of the guys were

younger than I, probably still in high school. Chet, as I remembered, was about my age, maybe a little younger. He seemed to be the catalyst for the group, and I could tell right away that he had marked me off his list of friends.

"What's Chet been doing the last little while?" I asked.

Laurie shrugged. "Mostly hanging around. He went to school a year or so at Las Cruces, New Mexico, but he didn't last long. He went mostly for the rodeoing. He does a lot of roping, and he is pretty good. He didn't like things there, though. I think he got lost in the crowds. He likes it better down here where he thinks he's 'top dog,' as you would say."

"Did he go on a mission?"

She shook her head.

"I thought everybody down here went on a mission."

She shrugged. "Oh, he talked about it once, but not very seriously. He's more interested in working on his dad's ranch and chasing off to rodeos in the States. And then while he's around here, he likes to play the big man in town. Some of the younger guys let him." Laurie heaved a sigh. "Don't let him bother you. He just wants to be impressive. I'm always hoping someone will come along and put him in his place."

I looked away. "I thought we were decent friends before. It's been a few years, though."

"He's learned to strut since then. Forget him."

"Does he have some kind of handle on you?"

"Nobody has a handle on me."

"Does he *think* he has a handle on you?"

"That's his problem."

"I guess he figures I'm here to horn in on all the local girls."

"Are you?"

I smiled. "Well, not all of them," I answered slowly. "He can have the rest. Besides, I just came to watch. The roping."

"Do you want to do some roping?" Laurie asked.

I shrugged.

"You're probably good."

"Oh, Grandpa taught me a bit." I smiled. "And I've roped a bit on my Uncle Dean's place. I haven't run off to join the rodeo circuit, though."

"If Jake taught you," she laughed, "you have to be pretty good. You're probably just modest. Jake knows more about roping than anyone. You know, if you want to try some roping, this would be the place. It's all for fun. Nobody's really good. Except Chet. Everybody else just plays around at it."

For the next thirty minutes or so I watched. The roping did look easy enough. No one was outstanding. There was more banter than roping. I would have liked to try it just for fun.

"You sure you won't ride?"

I turned to find Chet leaning against the fence again. I stared without replying.

"You're not afraid to eat a little dust, are you?" He chewed on a toothpick.

"I came to watch."

"Oh, that's right. You're with the girls today."

He pulled himself up and over the fence and dropped with a dull thud on the other side before I could think of a comeback.

Chet strolled over to his horse, mounted up, and took his position next to the chute while a calf was chased into place. Chet readied his lariat and pulled his hat down. He threw a quick glance in my direction and then nodded at Randy Hatch, who was running the gate.

The gate sprung open and immediately the calf bawled and bolted forward. Chet spurred his horse and raced after the calf, swinging his rope as he rode. The calf cut to the right and then to the left, but the horse followed, hardly breaking stride. It bore down on the calf, anticipating its every move, while Chet stuck to the horse like a burr, gliding effortlessly with each movement. Suddenly the swinging loop left Chet's hand and sailed over the calf's head, landing perfectly.

Immediately Chet pulled back on the horse's reins. The horse slid to a halt in a cloud of dust. Even before the calf thumped to the ground Chet was out of the saddle charging toward it. The calf kicked, fighting to get to its feet; but before its hooves could find the ground, Chet pounced upon it, lifted it up, and dropped it on its side. With his hands moving rapidly, he tied two of its legs and then raised his hands in the air. After his success was obvious, he untied the calf, slipped the rope off the calf's head, and let it scramble to its feet.

"Dang, he's good!" I heard Bill Romney remark as Chet retrieved his rope and sauntered back to his horse and swung easily into the saddle.

"Nice work, Chet," several of the men called out. I glanced in that direction. Calvin Cramer, Chet's father, leaned against the fence and beamed his proud pleasure. "Keep it up," he called out.

I licked my lips, insisting to myself that I wasn't envious. Chet made it look so easy. He was smooth, precise. I had never really wanted to be a cowboy; and yet, right then, for the sake of show, perhaps, I wished I could ride and rope like Chet Cramer. If only for a moment.

"I told you he was good," Laurie commented as Chet rode over to the fence.

I resented the compliment, although it was probably innocent enough, but it was as though she were suddenly siding with him against me.

"You sure you don't want to try it?" Chet asked me unexpectedly, panting and smiling. Bill Romney, Tom Cluff, and Benny Call strolled over as Chet asked the question. All grinning, they waited for my answer.

"Like I said before, I'm a little out of practice."

"Ah, it's just for fun," Tom Cluff said. "Let's see what you can do."

I wanted to joke my way out of my corner, but nothing I could think of just then seemed appropriate. I tried to laugh, even smile, but I couldn't. I shook my head and stared into the arena as another rider raced after a calf and missed his throw.

Dusk was beginning to settle in, and the men were getting ready to bring things to a halt. "This is your last chance, cowboy," Chet chuckled, staring down at me from his horse. "We're closing shop pretty soon." He rubbed his chin. "I'd at least like to see if you can climb on a horse by yourself."

"Go on, try it," Tom Cluff encouraged. I didn't detect any maliciousness on his part. "Nobody expects you to do what Chet did. None of the rest of us can. We just play around at it. Actually, we miss most of the time."

"I don't have a horse," I muttered lamely.

"Hey, we'll get you the horse. We didn't expect you to rope those little bounders on foot." The others laughed. Chet slid from the saddle and tossed the reins over the fence within my reach. "She's the best roping horse in Juarez. She knows more about roping than I do."

"He doesn't want to rope, Chet," Laurie butted in.

Chet raised his eyebrows and held his hands up. "Well, excuse me, Miss Wagner. I didn't know you were baby-sitting tonight. I didn't realize he had to ask for your permission to ride."

"Oh, just back off. He came to watch. Why do you always have to play the hotshot?"

"Why don't you just let little Jake talk for himself? He's a big boy."

Suddenly I was angry. I was angry with Chet for challenging me, but I was more angry with myself. I looked about me. Laurie, Cindy, Valerie, and the guys were all staring at me, waiting for me to either accept or decline Chet's challenge. I knew I could have avoided all this by never having made a pretense of being able to rope. But I couldn't change that now. And there was no way I would deny anything at this point.

"All right," I agreed. "I'll give it a try."

"You don't have to," Laurie said, glaring at Chet.

"Oh, by all means, get permission from Miss Wagner before you do anything."

I stared down the fence toward the gates, my insides churning and a warm sweat on my brow. In Mesa nobody cared if you could rope or ride. Cowboying was nothing to brag about there, but right then I did care about roping and riding. I wanted to. I wanted to bad enough that I was willing to toss my pride into the arena. I was even a little resentful that Laurie didn't have more confidence in me.

Laurie followed me. "You don't have to," she whispered.

"Don't worry. I've been on a horse before." I tried to laugh but managed to do little more than grunt. "I'm not planning to get bucked into next week. Just because I come from the city doesn't mean I don't know something about roping and riding. I've done my share."

Laurie returned to the others, and I stepped to the gate and pulled it open. Someone put his hand on my shoulder. I turned to face Grandpa.

"I thought you came to watch."

I shrugged. "I changed my mind."

"Because of them?"

I glanced toward Chet and the others.

"You don't have to prove anything," he said so only I could hear.

I returned his stare. "Who's proving anything!"

"You can't win, Jacob."

"I can do as well as most of them." I spit into the dirt. "Most of them missed. Anybody can miss."

"Chet's been roping and riding since he could walk. You've got a thimble full of experience."

"It's just for fun," I muttered.

"Is it?" He shrugged. "Suit yourself. But sometimes it's a long way to the ground."

I left Grandpa at the fence, marched over to Chet's horse, and swung up easily into the saddle. I impressed myself and gained confidence. Taking the reins, I jerked the horse around, letting it know from the beginning that I was in charge. I had read somewhere—maybe in a Louis L'Amour western—that a rider needed to do that. Immediately the horse seemed nervous and skittish. I gripped the reins more tightly.

"Loosen up, Jamison," Chet called to me. "Don't rip the bit out of her mouth. She knows what she's supposed to do. Let her do it."

I ignored the directions and kept a tight rein. If he said loosen up, then I'd keep a tight rein. Somebody handed me a rope. I made the loop and tried to get into position, but I was nervous and having a hard time keeping the tight rein I wanted and gripping the lariat too. My fingers twitched and my palms were damp.

"Tell us when you're ready, kid," the man at the chute called up to me.

I really wasn't expecting to rope the calf. All I wanted to do was to ride hard and look like I knew what I was doing. I could always blame my miss on the wind, a misstep of the horse, or the stumbling calf. I'd learned that much from watching the others.

I swallowed hard, took a deep breath, and nodded my head once. The gate burst open and the calf bolted forward. Even before I could spur the horse, she was moving. Her lunge jerked the reins from my hands and bounced me off-balance. I groped suddenly for the saddle horn but I overcorrected. The horse seemed to shy, and before I knew it I was tumbling to the ground in a heap, with dust exploding all about me. The taste of sand and dried manure filled my mouth.

"You all right, kid?" the man at the chute called to me, trying hard to keep the chuckle from his voice.

I ignored the question. I spit a couple of times and pushed myself to my feet, all the while hearing chuckles coming from the fence where Chet and the others stood.

My mind raced in search of something to say. There was nothing. Among friends I could have joked and soothed my injured pride, but joking was out of the question here.

More than anything I wanted to sink into the ground. I

didn't want to see anyone, speak to anyone, explain anything. I just wanted to be gone.

Slapping the dust from my clothes, and with shame burning on my cheeks, I stomped to the fence. I looked up once and my eyes met Grandpa's. He returned my stare for a moment and then looked away. I pulled myself up and over the fence and dropped to the ground.

"Are you all right?" Laurie asked, touching my arm.

"Yeah, I'm just great," I growled.

"You know, little Jake," Chet smirked, sitting on the fence, "you've got it all wrong. This isn't bronc riding. When you rope you're not supposed to fall off your horse."

I glared up at him.

"I told you to let the horse do the work. You were holding on to her too tight. She wasn't sure what you wanted her to do. All you had to do was—"

"Don't worry, Chet," I cut in. "I know how to ride."

He permitted himself to smile. "Oh, really?"

I turned on him, my fists clenched at my side. "What's that supposed to mean?" I flared.

His smile disappeared. "It was a question, *little* Jake."

"You're a big man while you're on a big horse roping a little calf," I said huskily. "Why don't you come off that fence and see if you can do anything on your own two feet."

"Jake," Laurie spoke to me, putting her hand on my forearm. "Forget it. He's not worth the bother."

I jerked my arm from her touch and continued to glare at Chet.

"Nobody made you ride," Chet shrugged. "How was I to know you were going to fall off your horse? I didn't figure you could rope, but I thought anybody could at least ride."

"Who cares if I can rope or ride?" I came back. "Where I come from only the lowlifes care if you can ride a horse or throw a rope."

Chet dropped from the fence in front of me. "Nobody asked you to hang around with us lowlifes. Nobody begged you to come to Juarez in the first place. You can catch the first bus out any time you want. And hope somebody's waiting for you at the depot in Mesa," he taunted.

"What's that supposed to mean?"

Chet shrugged indifferently. "You take it any way you want, *little* Jake."

Without saying a word I shot both hands out and hit Chet full in the chest, knocking him into the fence.

"Jake," Laurie called out. "Don't!"

"I wasn't looking for a fight," Chet said. "But if you think you make me nervous . . . "

"Let's go," Laurie said, tugging on my arm.

My hands shot out again and smashed against Chet's chest, knocking him into the fence a second time.

Chet hesitated for only a moment; then he charged, taking a punch at me as he stepped toward me. I was crouched and waiting. Oh, I was waiting, hungry for him! I took him by the wrist with one hand and jerked hard, ducking under his arm. It was a simple arm drag I'd done a thousand times in wrestling. While his momentum was still rushing toward me, I plunged my fist into his stomach. The blow doubled him over, but before he could drop, I grabbed him by the front of his shirt, stood him up straight and hurled him into the fence, then stepped into him and punched him a second time in his stomach. His legs buckled and he dropped to the ground.

I was reaching down to pick him up again when somebody grabbed me from behind. I staggered as someone tried to wrestle me to the ground. Pushing down with all my strength, I broke the grip and spun free, keeping my opponent's right hand.

I found myself facing Bill Romney, his eyes huge and scared. I lashed out once and caught him on the chin with a right punch. I was about to follow with a smashing left to his face when I heard my name. It was just my name, but the tone of voice, the inflection, gave me to know that it was a command as well. I turned to face Grandpa. His icy blue eyes bore into me. His jaw was set, his brow furrowed in anger.

Just then Calvin Cramer burst through the growing circle of spectators. "What happened?" he demanded, turning on me.

"He had it coming!" I snapped.

"Oh, is that right?" He started toward me. Suddenly Grandpa was between me and Calvin. Calvin stopped in his tracks. "Jake, I got some questions to ask him."

Calvin stood several inches taller than Grandpa and fifty pounds heavier, but Grandpa showed no sign of intimidation.

"Nobody can come down here and start banging heads without answering some questions, Jake."

"I'll ask the questions."

"Then I want to be here when you ask them."

"Where and when I ask the questions will be up to me."

For a moment the two men glared at each other.

"Get in the truck," Grandpa ordered.

As I looked out the side window of the truck to where Grandpa and the others were huddled around Chet and Bill, a cloud of gloom settled over me. I had just begun to think Colonia Juarez could be home. Now this!

I saw Laurie glance once in my direction and then look away. In total frustration I smashed my fist into the seat and slumped down.

It seemed forever that I sat alone in the truck. Finally Grandpa came, got in, started the engine, and headed for home. We rode in silence until we reached the bridge.

"They pushed me too far," I finally steamed. "They were just trying to make a fool out of me."

"They had quite a bit of help from you."

"They got theirs," I grumbled as we pulled into the driveway.

Grandpa turned the engine off. "Do you feel any better? Or did that just make you hungry for another fight?"

"What did you want me to do?"

"Do you try to solve all your problems with your fists?"

"I can," I snapped, jerking on the door handle and pushing the door open.

"I'm not finished," Grandpa called out before I had taken two steps. There was a piercing, commanding edge to his voice. I turned and faced him.

"I want to go in and go to bed," I grumbled.

"You'll go when I'm finished. This isn't Calvin Cramer asking the questions."

I was frustrated senseless, unable to understand everything that had happened. I wasn't a fighter, not like that. There was no way to justify what I had done; but with my pride smarting, that's what I tried to do. "What I did was my own doing," I came back.

"That's where you're wrong." Jabbing a finger in the direction of the roping arena, he went on. "Those are my friends and neighbors down there. Those are people I live and work with. A few weeks from now you'll pack your bags and be gone, but I have to stay. Ten weeks from now they're still going to be my friends and neighbors."

I glared at Grandpa. I had seen him somber, unyielding, and demanding, but this was the first time I had seen him angry, really angry.

"I don't like what's happened to your family any more than you do, but—"

"Don't bring them into this," I flared.

"And why not? You dragged me into your private fight. Do you want to start on me? Maybe I am pushing seventy, but I've seen more knock-down-drag-out fights than you'll ever dream of seeing. And I walked away from them with my teeth in my mouth and my nose unbloodied."

For a long tense moment the two of us glared at each other; then Grandpa heaved a sigh and relaxed. He nodded once, pushed open the truck door, stepped from the truck, and slammed the door behind him. "Chet can ride and rope as well as anyone around," he said quietly, the icy hardness gone from his voice. "But that doesn't make him a man. You can fight.

91

Maybe better than anybody around here. Maybe you could have taken Calvin on and whipped him good. But that doesn't make you a man."

"What would you have done?"

A smile pulled at his mouth. "For a starter, I wouldn't have fallen off my horse."

I looked away.

"I told you not to ride," he went on. "You were a loser before you ever got into that saddle. You were outclassed. That's why Chet wanted you to ride. He was baiting you. And you sank your teeth into his bait."

"He made a fool of me," I argued lamely.

Grandpa shrugged. "Five years from now you'll laugh about what happened this evening."

"He gave me a bad horse," I insisted. "He knew that horse would throw me."

Grandpa shook his head and leaned on the hood of the truck. "That horse is the best roping horse around. You could have held onto the saddle horn the whole time and Chet's mare would have run that calf down herself. She knows more about roping than half the men down there."

"Then why was she so jumpy?" I demanded.

"Because you were trying to ride her like you would a dirt bike. You were confusing her. She wanted to go after that calf. But you were holding her back. The horse wasn't Chet's fault."

Grandpa shook his head. "And the thing that's so crazy about the whole deal is that you wanted to impress that little Wagner girl. After you were finished, she wasn't impressed at all. But it didn't have anything to do with you falling off Chet's horse. Sometimes you have to fight. I know that. But not because you fall off a horse. And when you do fight, you better make sure you're fighting for a good cause."

"You have a good cause," I came back, still angry. "You've got people crawling all over your range, pushing you around, but you just sit back and talk. I won't do that. Never!"

I had no right to say what I did. I felt sorry as soon as the words were out.

"I guess I haven't decided whether the cause is good enough. I'd rather ask the questions now than jump into a fight with both feet only to find out later that I was wrong from the start."

We both stood in the growing darkness. Finally Grandpa pushed away from the truck and muttered, "It's late and we've got work to do in the morning. If you want to prove you're a man, let's see if you can stay up with me tomorrow."

# Chapter Nine

There were only a few streaks of dawn piercing the eastern sky when Grandpa and I left Juarez the next morning and headed up the river to put in a section of fence. It was just the two of us. We were both quiet, uneasy after the confrontation the night before. I suppose in our own reticent way we both wanted to say something in apology but didn't know how.

All morning we worked side by side, talking very little, just the bare necessities. The work was hard, but I was in the mood for it. Working gave me a chance to take my mind off home, roping, and fighting. And then there was the challenge Grandpa had dropped the night before about my proving that I was a man by keeping up with him. I was determined to make him regret those words.

I had never realized that pounding a few steel posts into the ground and stretching a little barbed wire could be so difficult. Of course, I hadn't taken into consideration the rocky ground, the heat, the thirst, the aching back and arms. I hadn't realized we were going to build the fence up the side of a brush-covered hill. And when Grandpa built a fence, he wanted it straight and solid, even if it meant hacking out brush or digging up rocks to clear the path.

By midmorning my hands, arms, and shoulders ached from pounding away at the steel posts, chopping brush with the ax, and battling rocks and dirt with pick and shovel. My leather gloves saved me from blisters, but they did very little to lessen the ache in my fingers and hands from the incessant jarring. I pushed on, struggling all the while to keep up with Grandpa, who seemed impervious to exhaustion.

As the morning progressed the sun climbed higher and became hotter, bearing down on us with a vengeance. My mouth was dry, my lips chapped. My eyes burned from sweat that poured down my face. But I pushed on, driven more by pride than anything else.

"I'd say about five more to go," Grandpa panted.

I looked up. He was pointing up the hill to another fence line that ran along the summit. "We'll join up with that other fence." He looked over at me. "Can we make it before we break for lunch?"

I swallowed and ran my tongue over my lips. The thought of five more posts made my arms and back ache.

"This morning if anyone had said we'd be this far, I'd have told them they were crazy. Maybe we should give you a rest."

It was a challenge. I gripped my shovel. "If you want to quit," I grumbled, "you can. I'm finishing what we started."

It was almost one o'clock when the last post was pounded into place and we staggered down the hill toward the truck. We tossed our tools into the bed of the truck and leaned there with our forearms on the sides of the truck, gazing back where we had been. Our naked steel posts stood in a perfect line, climbing up the hill through the brush, rocks, and yucca plants.

"Not bad work for a man and a boy," Grandpa commented.

"There's not a scrap of boy left in you, Grandpa. You're an old man, and you know it."

Grandpa spit and pulled the water jug from the truck. Unscrewing the cap, he offered me the first drink. "What were you trying to do, kill me out there? I'm not used to working like a crazy man."

I took a long drink and relished the cool rush of water. Grandpa took his turn. He was serious for a moment and then his face broke into a smile. "You know, Jacob, Martha would chew on me if she knew I was out here playing the kid again."

"Playing the kid?"

He nodded. "Trying to keep up with you."

"You were trying to keep up with me?"

"Well, I know I wasn't doing much of a job of it with my tongue dragging along the ground. But I was trying. Don't you ever let up?"

"And here I was trying to keep up with you." I laughed and looked away from Grandpa. That was the first real conversation we'd had all morning. It felt good. "I guess I can build fence better than I can rope. Maybe it's that I don't have to worry about staying on my horse while I'm swinging a pick."

Grandpa chuckled.

I shrugged, reached for the jug, and took another drink. I could feel my cheeks color. "I feel kinda stupid now," I muttered. I coughed and shook my head. "I guess I'm the first guy that's ever fallen off his horse like that."

Grandpa laughed. "No, Jacob, there isn't a cowboy around who hasn't fallen off his horse. However, most are lucky enough to do it without an audience." He pinched his nose and continued to chuckle. "I remember Vance Turley falling off his horse one year at our Twenty-fourth of July rodeo. A few weeks earlier he'd won himself a big fancy buckle out in Las Cruces, New Mexico. Us home folks were really expecting something big, but when his turn came, he drew this spicy runt of a calf that almost ran the legs off his horse. Vance charged after that calf, and halfway across the arena that critter dropped to its belly. Vance's horse stopped on a dime. But not Vance. He was still twirling his rope as he sailed out of his saddle, over the horse's head and even over the calf, and landed in a heap like a dropped sack of oats. That old calf kicked up its heels, tromped over the top of poor Vance, and headed for the end of the arena. You never heard so much hootin' and hollerin' in your life."

"I guess things wouldn't have been so bad had I not figured that Chet was just setting me up."

"There's always going to be somebody to set you up. You just have to be careful that you don't grab their bait." Grandpa laughed. The laugh started out as a deep rumbling in his chest and increased in volume until it exploded in his mouth. He rubbed his bristled jaw with the back of his fist. "I was living in El Paso when I started courtin' your grandma. I worked on a ranch out there trying to make enough dollars to come down here and buy a few head of cattle to start my own spread. I was as poor as a church mouse's country cousin. And about half as refined.

"I don't know what Martha saw in me. She was the prettiest girl I ever laid eyes on. Everybody thought so. The fellas hung around her like pigs at a trough. For some reason she took a likin' to me. Most evenings we sat on her porch and talked. She fixed me dinner whenever I was hungry. I didn't have enough money to take her fancy places. I wouldn't have known what to do anyway.

"The first fancy place I took her was to a big Gold and Green Ball." Grandpa smiled and shook his head, the color going to his cheeks. "I tried to get myself fixed up. I borrowed a dark coat and a pair of city shoes. But a feller can't hide ignorance under a dark coat. I was still a tall, gangling, bumbling cowboy with either my fists stuffed in my pockets or my foot crammed in my mouth. What I knew about being a gentleman you could have written on the back half of a postage stamp.

"I don't know how the fight got started. Martha was helping at the refreshment table and I was in a corner feeling self-conscious and out of place. I figured everybody was staring at me and waiting for me to act the fool. Then Roland Barnes strutted up, all fancy and clean, sporting a double-breasted suit with a red rose in the lapel. He was a banker and owned his own car and figured he was the cock of the walk. He'd even courted Martha and asked her to marry him. In fact, he still had his eye on her. He walked up with his big toothy grin wrapped around his silly face and slapped me on the shoulder like we were long-lost buddies. 'Howdy, cowboy,' he giggled. 'Fought any Injuns lately?' That's as far as he got. I knew he was up to no good, so I cranked back my fist and gave him a taste of raw knuckle. Why, I sent that boob flying over table and chairs. When he staggered to his feet, his nose was bleeding and his lip was busted."

Grandpa sighed but grinned. "Then the fighting started. Knock-down-drag-out style. I didn't know my fork from my spoon or how to put a proper knot in a necktie, but I knew what to do with myself in a fight. Then everybody ganged up on me, and before I knew it I was tossed out the front door."

For several moments Grandpa leaned against the truck without continuing. "What happened to Grandma?" I asked.

Grandpa smiled and shook his head. "She came out and got me. She told me I'd disappointed her, that if I was half the man she'd thought I was, I'd go back in there and apologize to everyone."

"You didn't do it, did you?"

"I married your grandma, didn't I? I would have rather tunneled through a mountain with a tablespoon than go back into that dance, but I knew if I was ever going to have a chance with Martha that's what I was going to have to do."

Suddenly Grandpa straightened up and announced, "Well, Jacob, we'd better get going. Your grandma will be wondering where we are. We'll grab a bite to eat and then get back here and stretch the wire. If you're up to it. You might have won the first round this morning, but I've got my second wind now. I'll work you into the ground this afternoon."

"You'd better take some of Grandma's advice and stop playing the kid. I let you keep up this morning, but I'll show no mercy this afternoon."

# Chapter Ten

"Are you going to the dance tonight?" Grandma asked at dinner Friday evening.

"Dance?" I asked, looking up.

"There's a dance at the academy tonight."

I took a deep breath and poked at my enchilada casserole. "I have a feeling I wouldn't fit in too well," I muttered.

"Oh, sure you would," Grandma laughed. "You used to run around with all the kids down here."

I glanced across the table at Grandpa. He didn't look up from his plate. Obviously, he hadn't said anything to Grandma about the fight. I cleared my throat. "I really don't figure any of them are too anxious to dance with me." I smiled.

"The girls can accommodate you. There's that Wagner girl and—"

"I don't think so, Grandma," I interjected before she could go on.

"You need to break away from your grandpa and do a little socializing. If you stick around with your grandpa much longer, you'll think the only thing there is to life is work." Grandma wagged her head. "Laurie Wagner will be disappointed if you don't go," Grandma added. "She stopped by today."

"Laurie stopped by?" I asked, looking up suddenly.

"She brought me a pattern from her mother. She asked about you, wondered if you were going. That's how I knew about the dance in the first place."

"She asked about me?" I tried not to sound hopeful, but I guess I failed because Grandpa looked up. He stared at me for a moment and then reached for a slice of Grandma's bread.

Two hours later I walked three blocks to the academy campus and headed across the thick, freshly mowed grass toward the gym where the dance was in progress. The evening was beginning to cool. I could hear the steady beat of the music wafting out from the gym. People lounged on the lawn in front, others strolled around the sidewalk, and some just stood about the doors, laughing and talking.

Up till now I'd been content to stay with Grandpa, ride horses, chase cows, build fence, and irrigate orchards. When I came home in the evening—stiff, sweating, and exhausted—supper, a shower, and clean sheets were the only things on my mind. But ever since Grandma had mentioned Laurie, I'd had a craving to break from my solitude. Loneliness made me bold, bold enough to go to this dance alone. It wasn't until that night that I began to understand how much I liked Laurie.

Hoping no one would recognize me right away, I ducked into the gym and found myself an inconspicuous spot in a shadowy corner. A few couples were dancing. Most everyone else was congregated in small groups around the gym, trying to talk above the music.

I spotted Laurie across the floor. Unfortunately, Chet Cramer and Bill Romney were on either side of her. Cindy Brown and Valerie Johnson were there, too. I stared for a moment and then turned away, discouraged. Loneliness might have made me bold, but not stupid.

I wondered if I should leave as stealthily as I had entered. Just then I spotted a Mexican girl not twenty feet from me. She had long, thick black hair that tumbled down onto her shoulders. Her light olive complexion was smooth, her eyes big, her smile wide. She was pretty. Beautiful, actually. I found myself staring. She glanced my way once, nodded and smiled.

I looked away, not wanting to stare, but a few minutes later my gaze drifted back to her. Twice more she caught me

102

staring. Finally I decided that I should either ask her to dance or keep my eyes off her. I chose the former.

As I approached, I heard her rapid, flowing Spanish, little of which I understood. I hadn't even considered that obstacle.

"Hello," I greeted, nodding once and stuffing my hands into my pockets while I rapidly reviewed everything I'd learned in first- and second-year Spanish at Mesa High.

The three girls stopped talking and turned to face me. None said anything for a moment, and I was about to launch into an unpolished Spanish introduction with a Portuguese twist when the pretty one smiled and replied in clear, unaccented English, "Hello, how are you?"

I grinned, relieved. "Well, what do you know. We won't even need an interpreter."

"What do you mean?" the girl asked, smiling.

I shrugged. "My Spanish is a little worse than poor, so I'm glad your English is better than good. Do you want to dance?" I pushed my fists deeper into my pockets. "I've been over there wondering why no one had asked you. Where I came from you would have been mobbed when you first came through the door."

"You probably tell everybody that," she answered. Although she tried not to, she blushed.

"I can promise you that I haven't told that to anyone tonight. Do you want to dance?"

She looked at her two friends, smiled and shrugged. One of the other girls laughed, jabbed her in the ribs with a finger, and turned away. The other friend said something in Spanish and followed, leaving the two of us alone.

"You're new here," the girl said to me as I led her onto the floor and we began dancing. It was a slow dance and gave us a chance to talk. "How do you like Colonia Juarez?"

I shrugged. "Oh, it's different. But nice."

"What brings you down here?"

"I've been here before. Lots of times."

"I don't remember you."

103

"My last visit was eight years ago. I'm Jake Martineau's grandson."

It was as though someone had turned off a switch inside the girl. The smile drooped from her lips and the light faded from her eyes. "So you're the one," she said, looking away from me. "I heard about your fight with Chet." It was definitely an accusation. "Do you go around beating everyone up?"

I sighed. "Actually, I don't go around beating anyone up unless they ask for it."

"They say you used to fight all the time. For your school."

"That's not fighting. I wrestled. Wrestling is different."

"I've watched them wrestle on TV."

"Oh, that's not wrestling," I cut in with a laugh, beginning to dance again. "That's all phony. We don't wrestle like that. We don't hurt each other," I said, wanting her to believe me.

The girl looked up at me. She wasn't convinced. "I'm sorry about what happened with Chet," I said, shaking my head. "Actually, we used to be friends. Good friends."

"I can see why you're not anymore."

"No, I mean when I used to come down here. We were friends then." I shook my head again. "Up at the arena I thought he was trying to make a fool of me. It ticked me off. Before I knew it, we were fighting."

The music stopped and we strolled from the floor, but I stayed with her. "Will you dance again?" I asked. She didn't answer immediately. "I'm probably not half as bad as you think. If you'll give me a chance I can prove that." She looked up at me, unsmiling. I waited a moment but she didn't answer. I shrugged. "Oh, well," I muttered. "Thanks for the one dance. I doubt anyone else would have given me the time of day."

I turned to walk away, but she reached out and touched my arm. "I thought we were going to dance."

"Do you know Chet very well?" I asked when we were on the floor again.

She thought for a moment and nodded her head.

"Good friends?"

She smiled. "I think so."

"How good?"

"Really good."

I rolled my eyes. "Just my luck. The first girl I speak to down here just happens to be good friends with the only guy I've had a fight with in years." I looked away. "I'm sorry. I guess I should have followed my first impression and stayed home," I grumbled.

"You don't look quite as mean as they said," she remarked, softening.

"Is that why you stayed and danced with me instead of ditching me out on the floor?"

She laughed. It was a musical laugh, one that made me want to laugh too. "You looked lonely when you first came in. You went and hid in the corner."

"And here I didn't think anyone even noticed."

"Of course, then I didn't realize who you were."

"Or you would have let me wallow in my loneliness, is that it?"

"Maybe."

"Well, I appreciate you giving me a chance to explain. Are you good for one more dance, or now that you know who I am do you just want to casually walk away?"

She shrugged. "Let's keep dancing."

"You know who I am. Who are you?" I asked.

"Magdalena Cruz. Most people just call me Mag."

"Do you live here?"

She nodded. "East of the Sorpresa. My father teaches at the academy."

"And you and Chet are good friends?"

"We see each other—sometimes."

"You weren't at the arena the other night."

"My brother was. He told me about it."

"So he's mad at me, too?"

"Not exactly. He doesn't like Chet. Or maybe I should say he doesn't like me to like Chet."

"So your brother is a fan of mine?"

"You'll have to ask him. You'll probably get a chance. He's been watching you for the last ten minutes."

I followed Mag's gaze and spotted a Mexican guy about nineteen or twenty watching us. He was short and muscular with his arms folded across his chest. He wore white pants and a soft yellow silk shirt with the top two buttons open.

"He doesn't look like a fan of mine."

"That's because you're dancing with me, not fighting with Chet."

"Well, I guess you're going to be able to introduce me to him. Here he comes."

"Hello, I'm Jacob Jamison." I held out my hand. He glanced at it and then shook it cautiously.

"Jacob, this is my brother Julio," Mag said, touching her brother on the arm. Julio nodded without enthusiasm. He had his sister's fine features, but his eyes emanated distrust instead of welcome. He muttered something to Mag in Spanish, which Mag tried to ignore. Not wanting to be part of a family feud, I turned to Mag, nodded slightly, and said, "Hey, thanks for the dances. I really do appreciate it. If you're free later on, maybe we can do it again. Alone," I added, glancing at Julio.

Without saying yes or no, she smiled and started across the floor with her brother. I watched Mag and her brother stroll to the other side of the gym. Still thinking of her, I turned and headed in the opposite direction, bumping as I did into Chet Cramer and Tom Cluff. They had their backs to me, and both of them turned around at the same time. I found myself on the periphery of Laurie's social gathering. Their conversation died, and the air was immediately charged with tension. I wanted to walk away but didn't know how to do it gracefully, so I cleared my throat and remarked, "Excuse me. I wasn't watching."

Chet glared at me without speaking. I smiled in a conciliatory way, but Chet wasn't accepting any apology. My eyes drifted about the circle of somber faces. I didn't detect any friendliness in any of them. My gaze finally settled on Laurie. She stared back coolly. Pride wouldn't allow me to just back away, so I blurted out to Laurie, "Would you like to dance?" I reached out and took her hand and pulled her onto the dance floor before she managed enough composure to protest.

My actions took everybody — especially myself — by surprise. I had her on the floor dancing before she caught her breath. For the first minute we danced without speaking. When the music stopped, I remarked, "That wasn't the warmest welcome I've ever had. But thanks for helping me out of there."

"So you just used me to get yourself out of a jam?" she accused. "Just a fill-in while you're not dancing with Mag."

"You still upset with me?"

"Shouldn't I be?"

"I lost my temper and made a dumb mistake. Chet wasn't exactly —"

"Chet didn't start the fight."

I shrugged. "No, I started the fight, but —"

"You said you weren't a fighter."

I rolled my eyes. "I just finished explaining all of that to Mag. Believe me, that's the first fight like that I've been in for years. I just freaked out."

"You didn't do too bad for yourself for not having any practice."

I heaved a sigh and shrugged. "There's not much sense in discussing it anymore. Actually I thought you might want to dance."

"What gave you that idea?"

I shrugged again. "I kind of got the impression that you had given me an informal invitation tonight."

"I invited you?"

"My mistake. I've been making a lot of those lately. Thanks again for getting me out of a jam." I started to walk away and then stopped. "I asked you to dance because I really did want to dance with you. If I hadn't wanted to dance, I wouldn't have bothered showing up. That was another of my mistakes." Before she could respond, I headed for the door.

"Leaving already?" someone called to me. I turned to face Mag. She smiled. "I was saving another dance for you."

"Thanks," I smiled. "I'll have to catch it another time."

"You don't like our dances?"

Suddenly Julio was strolling toward us. "I keep getting the impression that this is a closed affair," I said. "See you around, Mag. Thanks for your offer, though. I appreciate that. Believe me."

I left the gym and stepped outside, pausing for a moment in front to suck in a huge gulp of air. Burning inside, I slowly moved away.

"Jake."

I turned. Laurie was coming out the door. She hesitated and then came cautiously toward me. "Could I talk to you?" She chewed anxiously on her bottom lip and clasped her hands in front of her. I stared for a moment and then forced out a mean laugh. I felt mean. "Can I talk to you?" she asked again.

"You won't give me the time of day in there, but you'll sneak out here and talk with me in the dark where your friends won't see you. Is that it?"

"I'm sorry."

"I'll say you're sorry," I snapped. "This is the sorriest bunch I've ever seen. It's a sorry dance. And I'm sorry I showed up." I turned and started away.

Laurie reached out and touched my arm. "I deserve that," she said gently.

I stopped and faced her. Her eyes were misty. Slowly I shook my head. "No, you don't deserve that," I muttered. "I'm just burned."

"You have a right to be."

I shook my head again and looked at the sidewalk. "No, I'm sorry."

"I did invite you, Jake."

I looked up.

"I made a special trip over to your grandma's today. I looked for an excuse to go. And I told Martha about the dance and asked her to tell you to come. I would have invited you myself, but—" She shook her head. "But I haven't seen much of you. You haven't stopped by the house or anything."

"I didn't think you wanted me to bother."

"I did."

"So what was that all about?" I asked incredulously, pointing back toward the gym. "You acted like I didn't have any business even being here."

"I didn't invite you here so you could dance with Mag all night." She looked down at her hands.

"I danced with Mag because she was the only one in there that even gave me the time of day. You were off with Chet and his gang."

"He's a friend. Everybody's friends down here. You know that."

I rubbed the back of my neck. "Well, when I walked in and saw you there, I got to thinking that there was more to it than casual friendliness."

"I saw you come in."

"You did?"

She nodded.

"And you just left me standing there alone?"

"I was getting ready to walk over and talk to you."

"What stopped you?"

"You started dancing with Mag. After that I didn't think I had a chance." She shrugged. "That's why I was upset."

"But not in front of all your friends?"

"It didn't have anything to do with dancing in front of my friends. You got all wrapped up with Mag. It was like I was second choice."

"Would you go back in there and dance with me now?"

"I came out here, didn't I?"

I hesitated, pondering. "All right, would you like to dance? But the first guy that says one word to me . . ." I stopped, remembering Grandpa and his dance experience fifty years earlier. I chuckled. "I'll be sure to mind my manners. Do you trust me?"

"As long as you don't try to ride a horse." She bit down on her lip and giggled.

"You thought that was funny the other night, didn't you?" I asked, trying to sound stern.

"I did get to laughing a little once I got home and found out that Chet was all right."

I smiled as we started back into the gym. "Grandpa told me that in five years I'd laugh about what happened the other evening. I guess it was funny. From the fence. From the bottom of the arena it was just a little embarrassing. I can ride, you know."

"Oh, please, don't try to prove it tonight," she whispered, squeezing my arm. "You might hurt yourself the next time."

"I'll dance tonight."

"What have you been doing with yourself the last few days?" Laurie asked once we were back inside and dancing.

I shrugged. "Working with Grandpa. And thinking."

"About what?"

I looked around. Maybe I was just self-conscious, but it seemed that everybody was watching us. "You in the mood for a walk?" I offered. "I could use some fresh air."

"We just got here."

I shrugged. "It's a free country. We can just leave."

"Will you promise to dance with me under the trees?"

"I guess if that's what I have to do to get you to go for a walk with me. It can't be any more embarrassing than falling off my horse."

We strolled from the gym and wandered out onto the academy grounds. The moon and stars were bright overhead as we walked across the grass and under the giant maple and elm trees. For the first several minutes we were silent, content just to be together.

"Do you remember when we used to chase fireflies?" Laurie asked, taking my arm. "That one night we must have caught fifty of them. Our glass jars were like lanterns."

"I remember. We would come down here with Dad and . . . " I stopped. "That was a long time ago."

"I'm glad you came this summer," Laurie whispered. "I was beginning to wonder if . . . " Her words drifted off into nothing.

"Wondering what?" I asked. "Don't leave me hanging."

"Just wondering," she giggled. "I'm just glad you're here. It's fun to see a new face."

"Oh, so I'm just a new face?" I chided.

She shrugged. "Well, it's always nice to get some new blood down here. But I am glad that you're the one who brought it." She smiled. "I hope it's not just a summer visit."

I sucked in a deep breath of cool night air and dug my hands into my pockets. "It will depend on how things work out at home."

"Have you heard anything?" She paused before adding, "You don't have to talk about it if you don't want to."

I shook my head. "Mom's written a couple letters, but she doesn't say much about her and Dad. She's got a new job. She talks about that and gives me news about the girls. I think they're still trying to work things out. That's probably why she doesn't say anything. She wants to wait until things are pretty solid."

"What happened?"

"Everything just fell apart." I rubbed the back of my neck. "Dad did start seeing some other woman, but I think that's over. Now Mom needs to give Dad a chance. I think that's the hang-up."

"Do you blame your mom?"

I thought for a while. "Dad hasn't been fair. He's the one that — well, that messed things up. But that's over and done with. Mom's got to forget that if they're going to make a go of it."

"Could you forget?"

"I don't know. I really don't know. But," I added, somewhat bitterly, "if it's going to work, they've both got to do something besides stand around pointing fingers at one another."

I sucked in a huge breath of air and exhaled slowly. "I didn't come out here to talk about my problems."

Laurie squeezed my arm and pushed up against me as we strolled across the grass. We didn't say anything for a while. She leaned her head against my shoulder, and I felt a secure peace wash over me.

"You are going to ask me to dance, aren't you?" she finally asked.

I stopped. "Dance? I thought we came out for a walk."

"You promised that you would dance with me out here under the trees."

I laughed and looked around. "Well, I thought you were joking."

"Guess what?"

"Out here?"

She nodded. Though I couldn't see her face, I suspected that she was smiling, teasing me in a kind sort of way. "What do we do for music? My singing lacks something. It's about like my roping."

"Can you hum?"

"Not so that you could tell it was a song."

Laurie listened. "We can hear the music from here. We just won't be able to talk." She took one of my hands in a dance position and put her other hand and arm on my shoulder and behind my neck.

"You're serious, aren't you?"

"You promised."

Feeling a little uneasy, I put my free arm around her waist and muttered, "You know, you really are crazy. What if some-one sees us?"

"What if they do?"

"They'll think we've lost our marbles."

112

"Stop talking. I can't hear the music. And you're not exactly dancing yet."

The faint strains of music drifted across the darkened campus, and there under the huge maple trees the two of us danced.

We danced several times and then started to walk again without talking. I put my arm about Laurie's waist and pulled her next to me, and she pressed up against my side with her arms folded to fight off the slight chill in the evening air.

"I'm glad you're here, Jake," Laurie whispered, leaning her head against my shoulder. Her hair brushed against my cheek. It smelled good. "I was torn about coming home this summer. I didn't know why I finally decided to come. I think I know now."

We both stopped and I pulled Laurie in front of me. We were face to face, very close. I couldn't see her face, just her silhouette. I could suddenly feel my heart pound and my cheeks warm. I was glad for the darkness. For a moment we were just there, comforted by each other's closeness. Then slowly I leaned forward slightly and our lips touched.

"You're not nervous, are you?" she whispered playfully. "You haven't even looked over your shoulder for your companion."

"Do you always talk at such inopportune moments?"

"I'll shut up."

"Please do. How's a guy supposed to concentrate?"

"I've got to go home."

"Home? It's not even eleven o'clock. In Mesa you're a geek if you show up at a dance before ten-thirty. And you're talking about going home before eleven. Even Cinderella stayed out till midnight."

"I guess I'll have to be a geek tonight. I'm supposed to be home before eleven. I'm taking Mom to El Paso in the morning. We're leaving at 4:00 A.M. I'd rather stay."

"Here you get me all wound up, and then you leave me."

She was quiet and looked down at her hand that I was holding. "I was afraid I wouldn't see you tonight. I don't know what I would have done had you not been here. I would have probably dropped by Jake's house to pick you up."

"I like brassy, brazen girls. I should have stayed home," I said, laughing.

"You haven't been over much."

"I was afraid to. After my little disagreement with Chet, I wasn't sure you ever wanted to see me again."

"Are you still afraid?"

I shook my head. "Did you walk?" I asked.

"Drove."

"I'll walk you to your car."

I walked her to the car, holding her hand. We didn't say much.

"Where does this leave me?" I joked as I opened the car door for her. "It's going to make a short night for me, too."

"You can always go back in and ask Mag."

"Are you still jealous?"

She ducked her head. "Maybe a little. But I'll get over it. As long as I know you're not going to go back in there and dance with Mag."

I laughed, pulled her close one last time, kissed her on the forehead and whispered, "You don't have to worry about that."

After Laurie left, I didn't return to the gym. I had no reason to go back; and yet, I wasn't ready to go home. There were too many things going through my mind. I found myself wandering about the campus again, content with my own company, my own thoughts.

There was a bit of a breeze stirring from the south, promising to cool things off. I wandered around to the front of the main academy building and ambled up the front steps. There were two huge pillars at the top of the steps, one on either side. Between the top step and the front door there was a dark alcove. There in a corner I slid down along the cold brick wall until I rested on my haunches with my hands clasped together and my forearms resting on my bent knees. It seemed so private, the perfect place to sort through my thoughts. My mind skittered about, thinking of home, Grandpa, Laurie, Mom and Dad, Laurie, Grandpa, Laurie.

I closed my eyes. Before I knew it I was dozing. I awoke suddenly, hearing voices. They were low, coming from my left, one a boy, the other a girl. They talked and laughed and whispered, all the while approaching the front of the building.

I remained where I was in the shadows, not moving or making any noise. The couple stopped at the bottom of the steps close together, the guy with his arm around the girl. Slowly they turned and came up the steps, speaking softly in Spanish.

I stiffened. I didn't want them to think I was spying on them, but I didn't want to step out from the shadows and make them wonder what I'd been doing there all by myself.

As I tried to decide what to do, they reached the top steps and paused, facing each other. Their silhouette was perfect against the dim street lights, and I recognized them — Mag and Chet. I was surprised that they were together — and that they had managed to elude Julio.

Their arms were about each other and their lips touched twice. I looked away, feeling guilty. I couldn't help thinking of Laurie and me. I would not have wanted anybody to watch our moments together. But at this point there was no delicate way to excuse myself and leave. I was trapped. I only hoped they would hurry, and I figured that what they didn't know wouldn't hurt them. Besides, they were the ones who had invaded my privacy.

"Magdalena!" someone called in Spanish.

I looked up and glanced down the steps. Three male silhouettes approached. Mag and Chet jumped apart. One of the figures at the bottom of the steps moved forward up the steps, slowly, deliberately. I couldn't see his face, but I recognized Julio's short, stocky, muscular build.

For what seemed minutes, Julio and Chet faced each other. Neither spoke. Finally Julio said something to Mag in Spanish. She argued. He persisted. Then she took Chet's hand, held it a moment while she looked up at him, and hurried down the steps and disappeared into the night.

As soon as Mag was gone, Julio turned on Chet. A few mumbled remarks were made in Spanish. Chet spoke. There was more arguing. Finally Chet ended the discussion with a laugh and started down the steps. Julio caught his arm and held it. Chet shook his arm free, only to have Julio grab it again.

Chet jerked his arm free one more time, and then the animosity between them burst. Julio shoved Chet into one of the pillars. Chet was stunned for a moment; then he charged forward and took a blind punch at Julio. Julio blocked the punch with his left hand and sent his right fist crashing into the side of Chet's face. Chet staggered backward. He reached out to the wall to steady himself, and then he lunged forward. Julio put up his hands to ward off the charge, but Chet's rush was too quick. He smashed into him, sending him crashing into the opposite pillar. Before Julio could regain his footing, Chet was upon him. The two grappled in the dark, struggling for an advantage.

Chet finally managed to fight his way on top, pinning Julio beneath him. He grabbed the front of Julio's shirt, jerked him to his feet, and banged him into the brick wall.

The two at the bottom of the steps, who up until now had observed silently, sprang up the steps, grabbed Chet, and pulled him from Julio. Chet struggled to free himself, but the two held him tight, each clutching an arm and one taking a handful of hair and jerking Chet's head backward. Julio pushed himself away from the wall, wiped his mouth with the back of his hand, and approached Chet. Chet kicked at him. Julio dodged and then lunged forward, hitting Chet full in the stomach with his fist. Chet groaned and sagged limply. Julio was preparing to hit him again when I made my move.

"Back off, Julio," I ordered. "It was a fair fight without your two friends butting in."

I could hear Julio's labored breathing, but his face was only a shadow.

"If you want to take him one at a time, do it."

"It's between me and him," Julio argued in his accented English.

I glanced at the two who were still holding Chet. "Then tell them to let him go."

Julio spoke in Spanish and the two loosened their grip on Chet. He shook himself free and staggered toward the wall where he leaned over, clutching his stomach. "Thanks," he muttered at me.

My guard was completely down. I wasn't expecting anything when Julio was suddenly beside me. Without warning he sent his fist smashing against the side of my face. At the last instant I saw the punch and managed to duck slightly, changing what could have been a devastating blow into one that stunned me. The force of the impact snapped my head back and sent me staggering into the wall.

Lights exploded inside my head and a throbbing ache sagged at my left cheek and eye. As my head cleared, I heard scuffling at the bottom of the steps. Pushing myself to my feet, I bolted forward. Chet was fighting furiously to keep the three away from him. I reached the first guy, grabbed his arm, jerked him around, and pushed him back. Almost immediately Julio and the other guy turned and backed away from Chet, crouched and ready to defend themselves.

"That was a chicken's move, Cruz," I growled. "The next time you punch me, you'd better finish me off. Because you'll never get a second chance."

Gingerly I touched my cheek, which was still numb. I glared at Julio. He stared back at me and then sneered at Chet. "Are you going to hide behind him?"

"I can take care of myself."

Julio said something to his two friends, and slowly the three of them disappeared into the darkness. "Is that you, Jamison?" Chet asked huskily.

"How'd you get him so annoyed?" I asked.

He shook his head and pushed himself away from the wall. "He doesn't like me hanging around with his sister."

"He didn't like me dancing with her, but he didn't punch me out. Of course, you were doing a little more than dancing."

"Where'd you come from anyway?"

I shrugged. "Just be glad that I came when I did."

"You're the last person I expected to pull me out of a jam."

I shrugged. "I like to see a fair fight." I tucked my shirttail in and started away.

"Hey, Jamison," Chet called to me. "Thanks." I nodded once. "And Jamison," he said haltingly, "sorry about the other night."

I paused for a moment and then turned for home.

# Chapter Eleven

It was past 7:00 before I finally dragged myself out of bed the next morning. The whole left side of my face ached, and my neck and shoulders were stiff and sore. I grimaced as I looked in the mirror. My left eye was swollen and the skin over my cheekbone was puffy, scuffed and colored a deep reddish-blue. A dull ache that seemed to originate in the core of my brain sent throbs to the surface. I groped my way to the bathroom and had a hot shower. After that I felt better. My face still hurt, but at least I no longer felt as though I had just dragged myself from my own coffin.

"Jacob, whatever happened to your face?" Grandma gasped as I walked into the kitchen. She rushed over to me with a spatula in one hand and an egg in the other.

I grinned and shook my head. "It's nothing, Grandma," I answered, drawing away from her.

"Jacob, you look terrible. What happened?"

Sheepishly I stepped to the table, pulled out a chair, and dropped into it. "Just a little misunderstanding. Has Grandpa gone?"

"Have you been in a fight?"

"I'll be all right, Grandma."

I heard Grandpa's truck pull into the yard and the door open and close. Turning to Grandma, I said, "If I'm going to help Grandpa today, I'd better have a little breakfast."

"Not until I know what happened to you."

"It's no big deal, Grandma. Really."

"Let's see what your grandpa has to say."

Grandpa stepped into the kitchen, tossed his hat onto a kitchen chair, walked to the sink, filled a glass, and drank the contents. Then he washed his hands. He moved stiffly to the table, pulled out a chair, and dropped into it. Grandma stood at the stove, waiting for Grandpa to say something. He stared across the table at me for a moment and then asked, "You coming with me this morning? We have to take care of those orchards in the Tinaja."

"As soon as Grandma feeds me," I replied, looking at Grandma and grinning.

Grandma, waiting for Grandpa to comment on my face, glared first at me and then at Grandpa. When he refused to comment, she turned and dropped three eggs into the frying pan and pushed two slices of bread into the toaster. "You might ask your grandson what he did to his face," she muttered.

"Don't tell me you fell off another horse?"

"I was minding my own business."

"Chet Cramer?"

"Chet Cramer?" Grandma asked, turning around. "Why would Jacob have trouble with Chet?"

"Actually, I was getting Chet out of a jam."

"Helping him out and you fell in?"

I touched my cheek. "It's funny how things turn around."

"What is this all about?" Grandma demanded.

"Does Chet look as bad as you?"

I shrugged. "It was dark. He took a pretty good pounding, though."

"Over what?" Grandma asked. "What's been going on?"

"Chet can't handle his own problems?" Grandpa asked. "He's got to drag you in with him?"

"Three of them jumped him."

"And you wanted to even up the score?"

"I like a fair fight."

"Would somebody please tell me what's going on," Grandma cut in, exasperated.

"It was no big deal, Grandma."

"What made three of them jump him in the first place?" Grandpa wanted to know.

"Does it matter when it's three against one?"

"It might."

I took a deep breath. "He likes this girl, but her brother figures he's got to protect her against any guy that takes a second look. He's a fanatic about it. I had two dances with her myself. I mean, all I was doing was dancing and talking, and he was sniffing around like somebody's watchdog."

"Mag Cruz?"

"How'd you know?"

"Mag ought to stick with her brother," Grandpa muttered.

"But Grandpa, it was three against one." I shook my head. "Didn't you tell me just the other day that sometimes you have to fight?"

"The secret is to know when."

"All I wanted was a fair fight. Then Julio punched me. That's how I got this," I said, touching my cheek.

"I remembered someone saying something about turning the other cheek."

"I'm not used to turning my cheek."

"Try it. That second slap across the face tends to clear your head. It's surprising how well you think with a clear head. You can't right every wrong with your fists, Jacob. In fact, there aren't very many wrongs you *can* right with your fists."

"I didn't exactly turn my other cheek, but I didn't do any fighting, either. And I had every right after Julio punched me."

A smile cracked Grandpa's grave expression. He winked and remarked, "You're learning, Jacob. You're learning. Eat your breakfast. We've got to get moving."

"Is anyone going to tell me anything?" Grandma asked.

"I don't think it was much," Grandpa replied. "But Jacob

and I had better eat breakfast. We're wasting half the day just sitting here jawin'."

"He can't work like that," Grandma protested. "The doctor should have a look at him."

Grandpa looked at her and then back at me. "He should have thought about that last night. We've got work to do this morning."

The rest of the morning Grandpa and I spent at the orchards in the Tinaja. We checked on a crew spraying the trees, examined the progress of the fruit, jerked a pump out, tore it apart, ran to Casas for parts, and put the thing back together. We got so involved that we didn't even drive back to the house for lunch. That's the way Grandpa was. If he got involved in something, he wanted to stay with it until it was finished. By the time he realized that we hadn't eaten, it was three o'clock; and then he figured it would be better to just wait until supper before stopping.

After supper I walked over to Laurie's place to see if she was back from El Paso. Dusk was settling in when I turned up her street and spotted her lounging on her front porch in a lawn chair with a magazine in her lap. She didn't seem to be reading, though.

I leaned against the gate post and called out, "It must be pretty good reading to keep a girl home on a Saturday night."

Laurie looked up, saw me, and set her magazine aside. "Hi," she smiled, pushing herself out of the chair and coming down the steps to where I stood.

"All day I've been working and wondering if last night was real." I shrugged and grinned sheepishly. "I decided to wander up this way and ask you."

She ducked her head and reached out and touched the gate. "I was wondering if you'd drop by this evening." Her cheeks colored with a touch of embarrassment. "I mean . . . " She shrugged and smiled. "I am glad that—" She stopped in midsentence as she looked up. "Jake," she gasped, "what happened to your face?"

Instinctively my hand went to the side of my face. I touched the bruised cheek and eye with my fingertips. "I had a little trouble after you left last night."

"Chet?"

I laughed. "No. Matter of fact, I was helping Chet out of a jam."

"What was Chet's problem?"

"Julio Cruz and two of his buddies. If I hadn't been there, Chet would still be peeling himself off the front steps of the academy building."

I went on to explain what had happened. Laurie was quiet after I finished. Wrapping her arms about herself as though fighting off a chill, she looked out into the street.

"You don't seem too impressed by my gallantry," I laughed. "I was just trying to help Chet, and I caught an underhanded punch in the process."

"Julio was just trying to help his sister."

"She's a big girl. She can take care of herself."

"You in the mood for a walk?" Laurie asked suddenly.

"Sure. But no dancing tonight."

I took Laurie's hand and we started down the street. "Let's go down to the swinging bridge," I suggested. "I've been here this long and haven't even visited the famous swinging bridge of Colonia Juarez."

We walked in silence for a block, and then Laurie began to speak. "There's something you ought to know about Julio Cruz. About six months ago Mag's younger sister, Elva, ran off with an Anglo guy from El Paso. She was a year younger than Mag. It took the whole family by surprise. One day she was there. The next day she was gone. It was a month before they knew what had happened. By then she was alone in El Paso, and she had no idea where the guy was. He had promised to marry her, but that never happened. Right now she's living with her uncle in Chihuahua. She'll have the baby there."

"I didn't know," I muttered.

"Julio was the one who brought this Anglo guy to Colonia

Juarez. He was Julio's friend. They had worked together in El Paso. Julio introduced him to the family. Brother and Sister Cruz were never impressed. They worried about the attention this guy showed Elva, but Julio brushed it off. After all, this guy was his friend. I don't know what Julio would do if he ever found the guy. He's taken it pretty hard. He blames himself for what happened."

"If you ask me, he's just making things worse."

"Maybe."

"He doesn't have to take everything out on Chet. Chet didn't run off with Elva. He isn't going to pull anything like that on Mag. He likes her."

"Does he?"

"It sure looked like he did last night."

"I just know how Calvin Cramer feels about—" She hesitated. "About Mexicans. He'd never let Chet marry one."

"Marry one? Who's talking about marrying one? He just likes her. He doesn't care if she's Mexican or not."

"But Calvin Cramer does. And deep inside I think Chet feels the same way. Mag's just a pretty face, and Chet is out for a good time."

I shook my head. "I think you've got Chet all wrong."

"Chet has an older brother, Calvin, Jr. He married a Mexican girl. There wasn't a better girl around." Laurie shook her head. "Calvin Cramer won't have anything to do with the two of them now. Calvin, Jr., is working for a bank in Mexico City. The plan was that he would take over the ranch and orchards from his dad. Now they all go to Chet. But Chet can't make the same mistake his older brother made. I don't think Calvin even knows Chet is seeing Mag. If he did, he'd be furious."

"Chet doesn't seem the type to be afraid of his dad," I commented.

"I just know that Chet is looking after Chet Cramer. I like Mag. I don't want to see her hurt. Julio doesn't want to see his sister used."

We were quiet as we walked along hand in hand. We passed

the Sorpresa, which was just closing, strolled past the Catholic church and the town square. Finally we turned toward the river and the swinging bridge.

The swinging bridge, made of stretched steel cables and boards, spanned the width of the river. It had always held a fascination for me. I had loved to go there and stomp across, making the old boards creak and tremble while the one-hundred-foot bridge swayed back and forth and bounced up and down.

As Laurie and I crossed the bridge, I felt a lightness in the pit of my stomach. Laurie held my arm more tightly and pressed her cheek against my shoulder. I could hear the river below us. All about us were towering silhouettes of the cottonwood and sycamore trees.

In the middle of the bridge we stopped. I turned to the north and looked up the river. The moon was just beginning to rise, casting its reflection down upon the shallow waters below. From behind us began the careless, happy strains of mariachi music.

"I've always liked Colonia Juarez," I commented with a sigh. "Ever since I was a kid it's been—" I stopped and considered. "I'd forgotten how Colonia Juarez could change me. I'm glad I came." Laurie pressed against me. I enjoyed her warmth, her closeness, her understanding. "And," I added, pressing my cheek against her forehead, "I'm glad you picked me up the other day."

"As I remember, you're the one who stopped." She jarred me with a quick jab of her elbow and started to push away as though she were angry, but I held her and pulled her back. The moon's pale glow shone down on her face. I reached up and touched her cheeks with my fingers. "You've made all the difference," I whispered huskily. "A couple of weeks ago I just wanted to get as far from Mesa as I could. I didn't really care where I went, just away. Now I want to stay in Colonia Juarez. Not because I want to be away from some other place, but because I want to be here. The other day when I went to San

Diego with Grandpa, he said everybody should have a San Diego."

"San Diego?"

"San Diego is . . . what did he call it? His refuge. It's where he can put the rest of the world into focus. It sounded funny at the time. But I guess Colonia Juarez is like that for me."

"Jake's done a lot for San Diego," Laurie remarked. "He's done a lot for Colonia Juarez. Dad says he's glad Jake is here, especially with all the agrarian unrest and the tension down in Casas around the Paquimé."

"Your dad doesn't think Grandpa is dragging his feet?"

"Oh, he's worried about the agrarians, but he still thinks Jake's way is the only way that will be successful in the end. He certainly isn't a Calvin Cramer man. He thinks Calvin is just in it for the fight." She shivered slightly. "I worry about Colonia Juarez. I wonder if it can last. It's been . . . " She thought. "Well, it's been kind of magical. There's not a place like it anywhere. We have our own little world here, almost our own little country. Now everything is crowding in on us. Sometimes I get scared and think it won't be long before we'll have to leave again. I think of the first exodus, during the revolution, and I wonder if we'll be faced with the same threat. What would become of us?"

For a moment we were both quiet, and then I smiled and said, "We better not start philosophizing again. We don't have any Mexican pizza." Laurie laughed. "However," I added, "we could fix that soon enough. You in the mood for a ride to the big city of Casas?"

"I'm always in the mood."

It was almost 11:00 P.M. when I returned home. Grandma was in bed. Grandpa was at the kitchen table eating a bowl of bread and milk. I came into the kitchen and dropped into a chair across from him. "You waiting up for me?" I asked.

Grandpa shook his head but continued eating.

"Just hungry?"

Grandpa chewed for a moment and then shook his head. "Walt Shupe was over."

"Are the agrarians up to something again?"

"Building a few shacks. Nothing too permanent, but it's the idea."

"He wants to move them."

Grandpa nodded. "He's getting nervous. He's wondering if the rest of us are going to forget him, let the agrarians pick away at him so that the rest of us can keep our lands safe."

"Why don't you move them? You've talked. You've had time to think. Why not hit the camp hard and drive them off?"

"I don't like to jump in with both feet until I know where I'm going to land."

I smiled. "You don't want to charge in swinging."

Grandpa stared across the table. "Something like that."

I leaned forward with my forearms on the table. "Laurie told me about Elva Cruz," I remarked. "Did you know that?" He nodded. "Is it true about Calvin Cramer?"

"What about him?"

"Not having any use for Mexicans."

"He's got lots of uses for them. As hired help. He just doesn't want any Mexican grandkids."

"But he has some."

"Not in his mind."

I pondered a moment and then spoke. "Why is it that something can seem so right to start with and end up so wrong? Last night there was only one thing to do. Now all of that's changed."

"Nothing changed. You just see better."

# Chapter Twelve

The days rushed past. June gave way to July, and soon half the summer was behind me. Although in the mission field I had learned to get up early and follow a rigorous routine, this was different. It was so much more demanding physically. In the beginning it had been difficult for me to drag myself out of bed so early and go with Grandpa to chase cattle or to work in the orchard, but it wasn't long before I enjoyed that rough, hard life. I was anxious for the challenge and proud of the calluses on my hands, my tanned face and arms, my ability to keep up with Grandpa and Uncle Travis when we worked together. And we became a team, especially Grandpa and I.

When I first came to Colonia Juarez, it was to escape. I hadn't anticipated falling in love with Colonia Juarez. I hadn't figured on Laurie or a dozen other variables. Gradually Colonia Juarez became more than a quick stopover. It blossomed into home. My feelings softened and I looked forward to a whole summer here.

I spent most evenings with Laurie. We sat on her porch, strolled down to the academy, walked to the river and the swinging bridge. Occasionally we drove to Casas for a bite to eat or a movie. Sometimes during the day Laurie went with me when all I needed to do was run out to the Tinaja to check on the water in an orchard or to drive to Casas for Grandma or Grandpa. Having Laurie always there helped me forget what

I had lost in Mesa. But Laurie wasn't just a fill-in, an emotional balm to get me over a hard time. There was more to it than that. I knew that what had developed between Laurie and me wasn't going to end with the summer.

I really didn't know how things were going between Mom and Dad. Dad had never written or called. Mom wrote regularly. She sounded happy enough. But she had managed to appear happy when I was on my mission, and nothing was right at home. She never went into detail as far as how things were shaping up with her and Dad. Occasionally she mentioned something about Dad and his work, but I wasn't interested in his work. I wanted to know about the family.

I had started writing to Mom. I was pretty evasive when it came to how I felt and what my plans were. I didn't dare expose my deeper feelings until I knew whether there was going to be some kind of reciprocation.

During this time the agrarians were always with us. Whenever a group of men huddled in a corner at a social, congregated about a parked truck or tractor, or rested on their haunches in a field or orchard, they were almost always discussing in hoarse whispers the squatters.

Another group, smaller than the first, had moved onto Thomas Whetten's land, which only made people in Juarez more fearful and concerned; but still the town was divided as to what should be done. So nothing was done. Everyone waited to see if the governor would come to the ranchers' assistance. In the meantime, the ranchers waited nervously to see whose place would be next.

Although the squatters' camp was only a mile or two from Grandpa's range, Grandpa still hadn't been bothered directly. There were those, led by Calvin Cramer, who assumed that as soon as the problem struck closer to home, Grandpa would be insisting on stronger measures.

One morning during breakfast there was a knock at the door. Grandma got up from the table and answered it. Reese Taylor, one of Grandpa's neighbors, stood in the doorway. He was a big man with a huge barrel chest and an equally large stomach that pressed out against the bottom buttons of his shirt. When Grandpa had been bishop of the Juarez Ward, Reese had been one of his counselors.

"I'm sorry," Reese apologized as Grandma opened the door. "I didn't mean to barge in on you while you were eating. I'll just wait out by the truck until — "

"Oh, you won't do any such thing," Grandma insisted, taking Reese by the arm and pulling him into the kitchen. "Jake's almost finished. Have a chair."

Reese plopped down into a kitchen chair, crossed his legs, and hung his hat on his knee.

"Would you like a piece of toast," Grandpa offered, pushing the plate of toast toward him. "And some of Martha's black-berry jelly. She'll be offended if you don't," Grandpa warned with a twinkle in his eyes.

Reese fixed his toast and jelly and took a huge bite. "Did you hear about the trouble out at the Shupes' place last night?" he asked casually, chewing his toast.

Grandpa looked up. He stared for a moment at Reese without speaking and then slowly shook his head.

"Clyde Shupe got hisself roughed up a bit by that bunch of squatters. Him and a couple other kids, Chet Cramer and one of the Hatch boys."

"How'd that happen?"

"Near as I can tell," Reese explained, taking another huge bite, "Clyde and the other two figured on sabotaging the wind-mill. They figured that if those squatters didn't have water, they couldn't stay."

"They went right into the camp?"

Reese nodded. "Last night, around midnight." Reese wagged his head. "Crazy kids. Figured all they'd have to do is march into that camp, pull the pins, and walk out again. But those squatters had two fellers watching the place. They caught the Shupe boy. The other two hightailed it off into the brush. The Shupe kid got slapped around a bit. Took thirteen stitches

131

to put his head back together. Blacked his eye and almost broke his nose."

"Whose idea was this?" Grandpa asked.

"I don't know, but Calvin Cramer is foaming at the mouth. He's ready to head out there and clean the place out. There's them that would follow him. If you threw in with them," Reese added.

Grandpa didn't respond. Reese continued to eat, relishing the toast and jelly. "Last night was a bad night all the way around," Reese went on. "There was trouble down at Paquimé."

"Trouble at Paquimé?"

"A group tried to break in and tear the place apart. Luckily the state police were there. From what I understand it got a little mean. The police banged some heads, tossed some of that tear gas. They cleaned the place out, though. But things are pretty tense still." Reese shook his head. "Jake, if things get rough with these agrarians, we're not going to get any help from that bunch of state police down there. They have their hands full."

Reese finished his toast, then licked his fingers and wiped them on his pants. "I came over to see if I could borrow a few bales of hay from you. I was expecting a load of hay last week, but it hasn't come. I just need a few bales for my milk cow."

"Jacob, why don't you run out and help Reese get a load. Give him a ton."

"I only need a few bales. The other should be here any day now."

"Give him a ton," Grandpa said to me.

As Reese Taylor was leaving with his hay, Uncle Travis pulled into the driveway and climbed from his red Dodge truck. Uncle Travis looked more like an efficient banker than a rancher. Unlike Grandpa, whose features were rough and unpolished, Uncle Travis was handsome and striking. He dressed well, even when he was working. He was shorter than Grandpa, but he was more filled out and carried himself in an imposing sort of way. He was used to having things his way. When he asked a person to do something, he expected it to be done, or he wanted a good reason why it wasn't.

"Where's Dad?" he asked me as he came up. He was all business. There had never been a lot of warmth between us. Uncle Travis didn't seem to have time for that sort of thing.

Just then Grandpa came out the front door and walked toward us.

"We still planning to ride out on the flats?" Uncle Travis asked Grandpa as he walked up. "Checking my records last night, I'm almost positive that there's still half a dozen or a dozen head of cattle out that way. Probably over on that hilly section next to Shupe's place."

Grandpa rubbed his bristled jaw a moment, deep in thought. "Jacob and I were going to brand those calves up the river today, but I guess we can ride out on the flats and see if we can bring those other cattle in and run them up the river. There's better grazing up that way."

"You mean those calves up the river haven't been branded and vaccinated yet?"

Grandpa shook his head.

"That was supposed to have been done two weeks ago at the latest. I had a crew last week that could have gone up there and taken care of it. Why didn't you let me send them?"

"I promised Jacob I'd let him help me with that."

"Dad, we're not running a rodeo. Those calves needed to be vaccinated and branded."

"We'll take care of them."

"No, I'd better get a crew out there this afternoon. José Luís can grab a couple from the orchard and—"

"Travis, Jacob and I will take care of it," Grandpa cut in.

Travis stared at Grandpa. "Dad," he began to protest.

Grandpa held up his hand. "Travis," he said, smiling, "I'm still in this for the fun. I like to wrap my fingers around a branding iron now and again. Even if it's a couple of weeks late."

We didn't talk much as we headed out of Juarez and made our way onto the flats. The night hadn't really cooled things off. Already the morning sun was bearing down, warming things up for a real scorcher.

"I saw Guillermo Verdugo yesterday," Uncle Travis remarked as we rode along. Guillermo rented an old house from Grandpa. He had a large family and worked as a custodian for the academy. Grandpa didn't comment. "Has he paid any rent this month?"

"No."

"That makes five months in a row that he hasn't paid," Uncle Travis reminded Grandpa.

Grandpa patted his horse's neck and brushed at a fly that buzzed about the horse's ears. "Guillermo's done a lot for that old house since he moved in. He's fixed it up. Taken real good care of that lot, too. That place was in sad shape after that last bunch of renters moved out."

"He agreed to do all that when he moved in. That's why we charged him half rent."

"He's done more on that house than I'd planned for him to do."

"But he still owes us five months of rent."

"Oh, he brought me over the rent last week," Grandpa stated indifferently.

"I thought you said he hadn't paid."

"I told him to keep it, to put it into the house or the lot."

"What?"

"He's been having a hard time with his two young ones being sick and all."

"Yes, and you told the doctor to send you the bill."

"Travis, he's had a hard time. I can give him a break. I like having someone up by that north orchard. He keeps an eye on things for us. Last spring when we had all that vandalism up that way our place was the only one that was missed. He saved us a couple of years of rent that night."

Uncle Travis shook his head. "Dad, everybody's having a hard time."

"Travis, I'm not so hard up that I can't help a friend out when I want. What's a few thousand pesos?"

"If it was just now and again, Dad, but every time I turn around you're helping someone else out. Paco Pabón has an open account at the store."

"He's a cripple. Nobody else is looking after him. He doesn't buy much."

"He's not *your* cripple. Give someone else a chance to do a little charity. Don't hog it all for yourself. Whenever someone needs something, he's pounding on your door for help."

"And as long as I'm able, I'll give it to him. It hasn't hurt me yet."

"But things are getting tough for us, too."

"We're not down to the bone yet."

"Do we have to drive the knife clear to the bone before we stop cutting?" Uncle Travis shook his head in defeat. "Oh, all right," he sighed, "but I sure wish you'd find a different hobby. Charity is too expensive."

Nothing else was said. We found Uncle Travis's cattle in the brush and hill country bordering the flats. We worked all morning and into the afternoon rounding up fifteen heifers and steers. On our way back, driving the stock in front of us, we passed over a dry, winding *arroyo* and heard the bawl of a calf to our left where the *arroyo* disappeared into a stand of mesquite and yucca plants.

"Sounds like one of ours," Grandpa commented as we listened to the calf's cry. "And he bawls like he's got his tail in a crack."

Leaving the other cattle grazing on a few patches of grass, we turned our horses in the direction of the calf's bawl. The *arroyo* made a natural path for us, but down in its dry bottom with the mesquite on either side of us we couldn't see for any distance. So we depended on our ears, following the sound of the calf up the *arroyo* as it wound its way between two small hills.

Suddenly we broke from the mesquite into a small clearing about thirty yards across. Because of the arrangement of the hills and the mesquite growing everywhere, the clearing was completely concealed until we were into it.

I was in the lead and the first to see the small group of Mexican men — six of them — milling to the left of the *arroyo* on the edge of the clearing. Not expecting to find anyone out in this country, I jerked my horse to a halt. Grandpa and Uncle Travis pulled up next to me.

I spotted the calf, stretched out and struggling on the ground behind and a little to the right of the men. One of the Mexicans held a long knife. It was all too obvious what was about to happen.

Uncle Travis stiffened and jerked on his horse's reins. For a moment the horse fought the bit, taking two or three prancing steps backward. Then Uncle Travis growled and patted the horse's neck until it settled down.

Time seemed suspended as our eyes locked with the Mexicans'. We had caught these men completely off guard. Nothing moved, and I became distinctly aware of how stifling the heat was.

"Let's just back up real slow and head out of here," Uncle Travis rasped after our initial shock. "They've got us outnumbered."

"That's one of ours," Grandpa commented casually, nodding his head toward the calf.

"They might argue that point," Uncle Travis whispered hoarsely.

"I didn't come to argue."

"Let's not play the hero, Dad."

"You and Jacob wait here."

Uncle Travis's hand shot out and caught Grandpa's arm. "Dad," he hissed, his face chalky and drawn, "you don't know what those guys are planning. We're outnumbered. The best thing for us to do is just get out of here."

Grandpa slowly tugged his arm free, permitting a smile to pull at his mouth. "How we going to stay in business, Travis, if we don't round up all our cattle? You and Jacob wait here."

Uncle Travis threw a nervous glance toward the fidgeting Mexicans. "We could all get shot if they're armed. They're stealing cattle and—"

"Maybe." Grandpa shrugged and glanced at me. I returned his stare. My eyes felt as though they were going to burst from my head. Each breath I took was raspy torture. My mouth was dry and the palms of my hands were wet with sweat. I wanted to protest to Grandpa, but to protest was to reveal my fear, and at that moment I didn't want anyone to know how afraid I was.

Grandpa touched his spurs to his horse's flank and the horse climbed from the *arroyo*. Uneasily the six Mexicans began to fan out as Grandpa approached, their gaze going first to Grandpa, then to Uncle Travis and me, and finally back to Grandpa.

They were a dirty, ragged lot, all of them unshaven, most wearing rough leather sandals without socks. Their faces were gaunt; their eyes betrayed suspicion; their hands twitched. They had been caught in crime. They knew it, and they knew we knew it.

"*Buenas tardes*," Grandpa greeted with a nod of his head. He laughed pleasantly and nodded toward the calf. "*Hemos buscado este todo el día.*" None of the Mexicans responded. Instead they stared coldly at Grandpa, tense and cautious. "*Muchas gracias por encontrarlo*," Grandpa went on, shrugging.

Two of the men wiped their palms on their pant legs. All of them scowled.

Grandpa touched his spurs to his horse's flank again. The horse stepped through the sandy soil and stopped next to the steer. Grandpa dismounted a couple of feet from the calf. The Mexicans began closing in around him but kept a reasonable distance, always keeping an eye on Uncle Travis and me. Grandpa ignored them and they stopped, forming a jagged semicircle around him, his horse, and the calf.

Slowly Grandpa bent over, patted the steer's neck, rubbed its side and then gradually slid his hand down a hind leg where he soon worked the rope loose. The steer came to its feet. Grandpa by now had grabbed the other rope and was slipping the loop over the steer's head.

As the steer broke loose and started down the *arroyo*, Grandpa turned to the Mexicans and spoke amiably, as though he were visiting with neighbors rather than a group of cattle thieves. He seemed in no hurry to leave, but all the while my heart hammered painfully while I prayed silently that he would make a quick exit before the situation exploded and engulfed us all.

I don't know how long he talked, maybe a minute. Maybe two. At the most three, but it seemed hours from where I watched, choking on my fear.

"Jacob," Grandpa called to me, still facing the Mexicans. I jumped at the sound of my name. "Go back to where we left the cattle and bring back that little roan heifer we found this morning."

I looked over at Uncle Travis, not knowing exactly what Grandpa wanted. He chewed his bottom lip and returned my stare, then glanced at Grandpa, asking for a clue to the puzzle of his command. But Grandpa had his back turned and was down on his haunches, talking and drawing in the sand with a stick.

I pulled my horse around and galloped back to the cattle, all the while trying to sort out in my mind what Grandpa intended for me to do. I knew I couldn't afford to make a mistake. Was his order just a secret way to send me for help? Was he trying to get me out of the area before trouble started? I didn't know.

My mind was numb with the realization of what was happening. It was the twentieth century, but suddenly here I was, face to face with a group of rustlers who looked mean enough to murder all three of us and drag us into the brush for the buzzards to eat. How was I supposed to act? Did I run? Did I fight? I thought of Grandpa. He hadn't flinched or hesitated. Not once. There was never any fear, only hardened resolve.

Surely as Grandpa had ridden up to the thieves he had remembered that terrible experience fifty years earlier when he had almost lost his life. Of all people he had the right to be afraid, to leave the calf and race from the scene. But he had chosen instead to replay that horrible drama. I began to wonder if his experience fifty years earlier had given him a relentless courage. After having grappled with death once, perhaps he was immune to fear.

I found the roan heifer and headed back to where I had left Grandpa and Uncle Travis. Nothing had happened while I was gone. I drove the heifer into the clearing. Grandpa spoke a few more words to the Mexicans and then mounted his horse. He tipped his hat one more time and then galloped into the *arroyo*. Uncle Travis and I hurried after him, leaving the roan heifer with the Mexicans.

Grandpa reached the cattle ahead of Uncle Travis and me. He motioned with his hand toward the cattle and ordered, "Let's get these rounded up and headed for home. We're running late."

Uncle Travis sat stiffly astride his horse with his jaw clamped tight. "What about the heifer?" he suddenly burst out.

"What about it?"

"You know what they'll do to it."

"I gave it to them."

"What?"

"Let's get these cattle moving."

"They're the squatters from the Shupe place."

"Probably so."

Uncle Travis stared for a moment. In complete frustration he spurred his horse and began rounding up the cattle and heading them for Juarez.

"Dang!" I muttered hoarsely. "I was scared spitless. I thought we were all goners. I kept telling myself, 'This is crazy. I'm going to get shot down by a bunch of cattle rustlers.'"

Grandpa chuckled.

"Doesn't anything scare you?" I asked with unmasked admiration.

He looked over at me as he rode along. "Sure. Everybody gets scared. Some just show it more than others."

"Just what was that all about?" Uncle Travis demanded when he rode over to join us. Grandpa ignored the question. "Dad, what was going on back there?"

"A little exchange."

Uncle Travis raked his fingers through his thick black hair and then wiped his brow with the back of his forearm. "Dang!" he muttered. "I could just see myself hauling you back to Mom and telling her that I'd let you ride into a mess like that. You could have gotten yourself killed."

"My horse could throw me and I could fall and break my neck. But that doesn't stop me from riding."

"This is different and you know it. Let's just leave the cattle here and pick them up tomorrow so that we can get some help now."

"For what?"

"They stole our steer."

Grandpa shook his head. "How could they steal it? It was still on our land. They hadn't harmed it."

"But they have the heifer now."

Grandpa rubbed his jaw. "They were hungry," he replied simply. "I gave them the heifer."

"Half of Mexico is hungry," Uncle Travis snapped. "You can't feed the whole country, Dad."

Grandpa faced Uncle Travis. "I happened to have enough to feed that little bunch."

"Dad," Uncle Travis argued, "you can't walk around with a bleeding heart. They stole that steer."

140

Grandpa shook his head. "It wasn't stolen. We would have never proved they did."

"But you know good and well that, had we showed up five minutes later, you could have helped them cut it up."

"We didn't come five minutes later."

"They ended up with another one. That little heifer was better than the steer they had. If you were going to give something away, why didn't you let them keep the steer? Why didn't you ride away from them to start with and let them have what they'd already stolen?"

Grandpa smiled.

"Dad, I can't figure you out. You ride in there, risk your life, and get the steer. Then you turn right around and give them a heifer. Why?"

Grandpa heaved a sigh. "What did you want to do?"

"I would have taken the steer and kept it," Uncle Travis insisted.

Grandpa chuckled and shook his head. There was a teasing twinkle in his eyes. "No, Travis, you wanted to back out of there and hightail it back here. Empty-handed. That's what you suggested. We would have lost the steer had we done it your way. I'd rather give a heifer than have someone steal my steer." Grandpa was silent a moment, and then he continued. "Travis, I can do anything I want with my cattle. If I want, I can sell them. If I want, I can give them away. But I hate to have them stolen."

Uncle Travis shook his head in frustration. "Dad, not two miles from here there's an agrarian camp. That bunch was from there. Right now those agrarians are on Shupe land, but our land borders Shupe land. Now those guys will walk away from here thinking we're a bunch of pushovers, that they can take what they please. We could be next."

"I hope not."

"Dad, we should have taken that steer. This is our land. Nobody's going to take it. Those are our cattle and nobody has a right to go out and butcher them. And if anybody does, then

141

we've got to come down hard on them, so hard that they'll wish they'd never crossed over the line."

"You've been listening to Calvin Cramer too long."

"Calvin Cramer isn't getting his cattle butchered and a bunch of squatters sneaking onto his land. They know better than to creep onto his land. If we're not careful we'll get run clear out of the country."

"If we're not careful, we'll end up like Calvin Cramer. I'd rather lose my land than my character."

"There's only a trickle of them now," Uncle Travis went on, scarcely listening, "but if a wave ever sweeps in here, it will wash us all away."

"If the wave comes," Grandpa answered grimly, "it's not going to make a bit of difference whether or not I gave those poor beggers one of my heifers."

"But, Dad—"

"Travis," Grandpa cut in, "have you ever wondered what it's like to live like they live, not sure where the next meal is coming from? Did you bother to look into their faces? Or did you have your mind wrapped around one steer?"

"Dad, we've worked for everything we've got. We've earned it fair and square."

"I don't deny that," Grandpa said. "We've got it good, though. Most of our cattle is sold in the States and we bring home dollars. If at the end of the year the peso is a thousand to one to the dollar, we won't be hurting too bad. If the peso drops before we sell our fruit, we just raise the price of our fruit. But those men back there can't do that. When prices go up, all they can do is cut back. Well, they've been cutting for a lot of months. They're down to bare bone. Their kids are hungry. They look out here and see our big ranch and our cattle. They know we live in big houses. We're not hurting."

"We're pinched, too," Uncle Travis argued. "It hasn't been easy for us."

"Our hard times, our very worst times, would be their prosperity. What's one lousy steer or heifer to us?" Grandpa's eyes bore into Uncle Travis, but Uncle Travis didn't flinch. "With a change of circumstances, that could be you and me out there getting ready to butcher somebody's steer. That could be us squatting on somebody's land."

"Would you steal somebody else's steer?" Uncle Travis shot back. For a long time the two of them stared at each other without speaking.

Finally Grandpa shrugged. "I'm glad I'm still in a position to give my heifers away rather than having to steal them from someone else. But if the time ever comes that I'm there, I hope someone rides along that can give me a heifer."

"Dad, there was a time when you'd have banged heads together and ridden out of there with your steer. You wouldn't have looked back once. And you wouldn't have sent them a heifer in return."

Grandpa leaned heavily on his saddle horn. "Maybe I'm getting soft," he replied, not looking at Uncle Travis. "Maybe I'm just getting old and soft. Or maybe I've spent too many nights, staring up at the ceiling, wondering about fellows like those back there. And after I think about them long enough, I don't begrudge a heifer or two. I hate a thief. But I hate to see a man starve."

"And it doesn't bother you to lose your land?"

Grandpa sighed and looked at him. His land stretched in all directions. He studied it. "I've worked a lifetime for this. I've poured sweat and blood into this land. I don't want to give it up. I used to think it was my whole life." He shook his head. "I was wrong, Travis. I was wrong."

# Chapter Thirteen

That evening a little after six o'clock, Grandpa, Uncle Travis, and I were just finishing putting the cattle in the corral when a pickup pulled into the driveway and skidded to a halt. Milton Romney, Benny Hatch, and Calvin Cramer stepped out, dragging and pushing a young Mexican, who was barely out of his teens. The top buttons of his shirt had been torn off and his shirttail was hanging out. His eyes, dark with anger and hate, stared out from a lean face. He was like a trapped animal. His eyes darted about, searching for an escape.

Calvin Cramer dragged the fresh, bloody hide of a roan calf from the back of the truck and dropped it in the gravel in front of the Mexican. Glaring at the Mexican, he spoke to Grandpa. "I don't know where the heifer is that was wearing that, but this fella sure does." Pointing down at the hide, Calvin went on. "That cow belonged to you, Jake. This joker and his friends — we couldn't catch the others — butchered one of your calves. It carries your brand." Milton Romney and Benny Hatch, with their eyes on the Mexican, nodded emphatically.

I stared at Grandpa. He studied the hide, examining it until he found the brand. Then he let the hide drop to the ground again. "It was mine all right."

"He's a squatter," Calvin declared. "If we didn't have an excuse to chase those squatters off before, we sure have one now. They're stealing cattle, and we've got proof. Now we can move."

"He claims you gave it to him," Benny Hatch said, laughing.

"Maybe you can set the story straight," Calvin said without taking his eyes from the Mexican.

"He's telling the truth," Grandpa said, straightening up. "I gave them the heifer. This afternoon."

All eyes turned to Grandpa, and a heavy silence descended.

"What was that?" Calvin questioned incredulously, squinting toward Grandpa.

"I gave them the heifer."

Calvin grabbed the Mexican by the left arm and jerked him forward. Still holding his arm, Calvin jabbed a finger under the Mexican's nose and growled at Grandpa, "Jake, this is one of them squatters. I'm sure of it. And you gave him a heifer to butcher?"

Grandpa nodded once.

Calvin released his grip on the man's arm. He faced Grandpa. "What do you mean, you gave it to him?"

"I gave it to them."

"What for?"

"They were hungry."

For a long time Calvin stared into Grandpa's eyes. Grandpa didn't blink. "We figured we were doing you a favor. It took us an hour to chase this kid down."

"I appreciate your concern."

"I'll bet. Next time we won't be so anxious. Here the rest of us are trying to get rid of those squatters, and you're trying to feed them."

"Just because I don't want them to move onto my land doesn't mean I have to hate them."

"Well, you'd better hate them or they're going to be camped in your backyard and living out of your kitchen. Then you'll never move them." Suddenly he turned on Uncle Travis. "Is that the way you run your ranch, Travis?" he demanded.

The question took Uncle Travis off guard. His mouth dropped open in surprise and then snapped shut. "Dad said we gave them the heifer. We do what we want with our own cattle, Calvin," he said.

"So you and Jake are together on this?"

Uncle Travis's cheeks colored. I could tell he was angry. "Dad and I don't see eye to eye on everything. But we'll work out our differences between us. We sure as heck won't answer to you one way or the other. And if we ever decide to give our whole herd away, we'll do it."

"You'd be stepping on some other people's toes."

"Then don't get your feet in the way."

Calvin turned and stomped back to his truck. Benny and Milton followed him. The truck engine roared. Calvin jammed the truck into gear and backed out of the driveway, stirring up dust and gravel as he drove.

The Mexican was left behind. Grandpa reached down, picked up the hide, and handed it to the young man. For a moment he didn't know what to say.

"*Es suyo,*" Grandpa explained.

Slowly the young man reached out and took it. "*Gracias, señor,*" he mumbled.

Grandpa nodded. "*Tiene familia?*" he asked.

"*Esposa y niña,*" he answered guardedly.

Grandpa nodded. The two looked at each other. The hate had disappeared from the young man's face and eyes. He became a person rather than a cornered animal. I hardly recognized him as the same man Calvin had dragged from the truck.

The Mexican took his hide and headed up the driveway. Grandpa watched him go. In fact, he stood staring even after the young man had disappeared. Finally he said, as much to himself as to Uncle Travis and me, "Mexico is full of young men like that. Young men with a wife and kid. And no way to support them properly." He shook his head. "I wish I had more roan heifers."

"Thank you, Travis," Grandpa said when we were all in the barn, putting away our saddles and bridles.

147

Uncle Travis tossed his saddle over a post and turned on Grandpa. "I don't answer to Calvin Cramer," he snapped. "And I won't have him coming around telling us how to run things." Travis tossed his bridle over the saddle horn. "I don't like giving cattle away either. But that's between you and me."

"Let's keep it that way."

"But if I had my way, I'd get a group and march out on that camp and drive every last one of them off the range. And I'd post men out there in the flats, and the first time a group of those agrarians tried to move out there, I'd run them clear out of the territory. That's what I'd do."

Grandpa smiled. "I'm glad you don't do it. It would make me look mighty funny." He turned and left the barn.

Uncle Travis watched him go. He sucked in a deep breath of air, shook his head, and dropped onto a bale of straw. "I'll never figure him out, Jacob," he sighed. "Sometimes I think I know him, and then he pulls something like he did today and I don't have a clue as to what's going on inside his head." He looked over at me. "He can be a mean old guy when he wants to be." He laughed. "Once when I was a kid, there was a big Mexican fellow that came around to break one of our horses. Everybody called him Chino. Well, he started on one of Dad's horses. Chino was a mean one with a horse. He would break a horse's spirit and then ride him. Dad showed up and saw what he was doing to a little mare of his. Dad didn't ever treat his horses like that. He blew up. He charged into that corral and bodily threw Chino out."

Uncle Travis laughed and walked over and dropped down onto a bale of straw. "Chino wasn't used to that kind of treatment. From anybody! He came charging after Dad. I was only about eleven then, but I thought for sure Mom was going to be a widow when Chino was finished." He shook his head. "I didn't know Dad. I'd heard rumors that Dad was a mean guy in a fight, rumors about his younger years, but until I saw what he did to Chino, I had no idea how good he was. Chino didn't stand a chance. It wasn't even a fight. It was over and done with before it had begun."

"Do you think Grandpa ought to do the same thing to the agrarians?"

"Sometimes."

"You'd ride out with Calvin, right now?"

Uncle Travis smiled weakly. "I can say I would, because if I say I'll ride out there, I'm just deciding for one person. The day Dad says to mount up and ride out to that squatters' camp and drive those agrarians off the range, everybody in Juarez will follow him. Calvin Cramer knows that. I think that grates on him. Dad has to walk a pretty straight line, because when he decides to go, he decides for the whole town."

# Chapter Fourteen

Mom called on a Tuesday morning during breakfast.

"It's your mother," Grandma called over her shoulder. She sounded excited. I looked up from my scrambled eggs, hash browns, and bacon and stared at the phone. I hadn't received a letter from Mom for almost two weeks, which was unusual.

Slowly I pushed my chair back and walked over to the phone and Mom. In a way I was afraid to talk to her. Our last farewell at the border had left us strangers of sorts. I had never shaken the guilt I felt for having been so cold and indifferent toward her when she really needed me.

"Hello, Mom," I said with a guarded tone of voice.

"Hello, Jacob, how are you?"

I could tell she was trying to sound cheerful. I shrugged. "Oh, I'm alive."

There was a pause. "I was thinking about you this morning." She laughed, but the laugh was tense and lacked humor. "I thought I'd give you a call and see how things were going." She forced her laugh again.

"Just fine. No complaints. Grandpa keeps me busy. Grandma keeps me fed."

"I've been meaning to call."

There was another pause.

"How is everything?" I asked, groping for something — anything — to fill the gaps of silence. I swallowed. "How are you and Dad?" I finally blurted. "Is Dad there?" I asked, not because I wanted to talk to him but because I felt I needed to ask.

Mom was quiet for several seconds. For a moment I wondered if she was still on the line. "Dad isn't here," she finally said, just above a whisper. "He hasn't been here for—" She cleared her throat. "Since the week you left," she added hurriedly.

"What do you mean?" I asked. My voice was hoarse.

"I'm sorry, Jacob. I've been meaning to tell you. I knew you needed to know. I just haven't known how."

Everything was spinning. I suppose everyone else looking on could have told me this would happen. Perhaps to everyone else it was obvious, a foregone conclusion. It's strange that I had never considered it myself. Maybe I simply refused to let myself consider it. I just didn't want to admit that our family, which meant so much to me, could have absolutely no meaning for Dad. "What's going to happen? I mean—"

"Jacob," Mom cut in gently, "your father wants to marry Liz Carroll. He will as soon as the divorce is final. That's where he's staying. That's where he's been staying since he left. There was nothing to save. It was all gone before you left. I guess I should have told you that. But I couldn't. Not with you coming off your mission and all. I wanted that to be a happy time for you. I wanted you to have a taste of home, even for a little while, before it was all snatched away again. I'm sorry, Jacob." She paused.

"Marry her?"

"That's what he's wanted to do all along. I asked him to wait, at least until you returned from Brazil, just to see if that is what he really wanted."

Suddenly my mind was a total scramble. I didn't want to hear any more. It had been so much easier when I had clung to the security of my ignorance and illusions. But Mom's phone call was ruining all that, taking all the pretend out of my world.

I suppose I should have known. A man wasn't excommunicated because he argued with his wife or flirted with another woman.

I took a deep breath, slowly exhaled. "Well, I'm fine down here," I said abruptly. "You don't have to worry about me. I'm having a great time."

"Jacob, I wanted things to work out. I really did. Not for me, but for you and the girls. I just—"

"I know you did, Mom," I said, cutting her off. "I don't blame you. I was just hoping for . . . " The words vanished. I didn't know what to say. I ended up saying something inane. "Well, I better let you go. Grandpa and I have a lot of work to do. Thanks for calling."

It was a blunt way to end the conversation, but at the time, still reeling from the shock, I wasn't thinking clearly.

I hung up the phone. More than anything I wanted to be alone. I didn't want to have to talk to anyone. To explain things to anyone. At least not until I had had a chance to sort through things for myself.

I stepped back to the table and stared down at my unfinished breakfast. Grandpa and I were planning to go upriver and do the branding and vaccinating Uncle Travis had been nagging us about. I had looked forward to that, but now I just wanted to escape. My appetite was gone. I pushed my chair in and started for the side door.

"Aren't you going to finish your breakfast?" Grandma called after me.

"I'm not hungry," I muttered.

"But, Jacob, you have to eat something. I won't let you go until you've finished your breakfast. You'll—"

"Martha," Grandpa cut her short, "let him go."

The rest of the morning I walked. I strolled along the river, down in the trees and willows where I could find privacy. I wandered up to the Academy grounds. I hiked up the hills west of town and then ambled through some of Grandpa's orchards.

It was strange. As much as I had pondered my family's

situation, I had allowed myself to remain naive where Dad was concerned.

In the beginning the rejection hurt. But as the morning dragged on and I began to understand what Mom had known or suspected all along, I became angry. I wanted to lash out, to punish. Before the morning was out, I hated him. All I could think of was ways I could hurt Dad. I wanted him to feel pain and rejection. I wanted him to suffer. I wanted this Liz Carroll to suffer. And I wanted to be the one to cause this suffering for both of them. I wanted Dad blocked out of my life completely. I would never include him in my life. Marriage, college, graduation, work, his grandkids — these would all be kept from him. He didn't deserve any of them.

During the early hours of the afternoon I was hiking southwest of town, headed in the direction of the flats. I was calmer now, more calculating. My hate was stronger.

"Hey, Jamison, what you doing out this way?" a voice called out to me as a truck pulled beside me. I had been vaguely aware that a vehicle was approaching. I'd paid no attention to it. I turned. There was Chet Cramer in his father's pickup. Randy Hatch was riding with him. I was surprised by their sudden appearance and didn't say anything for a moment.

"You lost, Jamison?" Chet asked, grinning.

I looked around me and realized I was several miles from town. Shrugging, I shook my head and answered, "No, I'm just wandering around, doing some thinking. What are you two up to?" Since I had stepped in to help Chet at the dance, we had been friendly. Not like earlier years, but we could visit. And that had thawed things between me and the other guys in Colonia Juarez.

"Randy and I were out doing a little target practice. We're headed back. Want a ride?"

Before I could answer, Randy opened the door and slid over to make room for me. I stepped around the rear of the truck and slid in next to Randy.

"You're a long way out. You walk all this way?" Chet asked as I climbed in. I nodded.

"Jake sure keeps you busy. But I guess there's not much else to do down here. Unless you go out and hassle the squatters occassionally."

I glanced over at Chet. "From what I heard, the squatters hassled you."

Chet shook his head. "That was all Clyde's fault. He didn't use any smarts. He walked in there like a bull elephant. Those guys didn't touch me, though. About the time they would have pushed me around, my old man would have been out there banging some heads together. If those guys were on our range, Dad would have run them off a long time ago."

Chet paused before adding, "Jake's too careful. Maybe he's just afraid and doesn't want to get shot up again."

"Grandpa's not afraid."

Chet shrugged. "Maybe." He laughed. "According to my Uncle Walt, Jake had blood in his eyes when he found out nobody had done anything to the ones that shot him and his brother. I wouldn't be surprised if he evened the score. Jake didn't forget garbage like that back then."

"What do you mean?"

Chet shrugged as he drove along. "There are ways to even the score." He thought for a moment. "My old man had an uncle that lived up in Colonia García. That's up in the mountains. This was thirty, forty, maybe even fifty years ago. His oldest kid was killed by Mexicans in some kind of brawl. Uncle Martin claimed he'd get even. He was a mean one after that. Wouldn't have nothing to do with Mexicans. Wouldn't even let them work around him.

"A while before he died, he claimed he'd evened the score. He claimed that over the years he had ambushed Mexicans as they came down out of the mountains. He just shot them, dragged them out in the brush, and left them there. Nobody ever found out."

"You mean people he didn't even know?"

"That's what he claimed. That's how much he hated Mexicans. Any Mexicans." Chet shook his head. "He couldn't even remember how many he'd killed. Maybe as many as a dozen."

"Grandpa would never do anything like that."

"I don't know," Chet countered. "Those Mexicans killed Jake's brother. Just shot him down like a stray dog. They shot Jake, too. Left him to die. The police didn't do anything. Wouldn't that make you mad? Wouldn't you want to get even?"

I shrugged.

"Dad thinks he settled the score. My old man doesn't think Jake's as big on Mexicans as he makes people think."

"Grandpa wouldn't kill anybody."

"There are other ways."

"This uncle of your Dad's, do you think he could get away with anything like that?" I asked.

"It was wild up in those mountains back then. It still is. Have you ever been up there?"

I shook my head. "Mom talks about visiting relatives up there when she was younger."

"There used to be some Mormon colonies there. Not anymore. It's just dirt road back in there. It's pretty, though. We used to go up there all the time. Now it's mean and wild. There's a lot of drug traffic out of the mountains."

"Drugs?" I asked.

"They grow a lot of marijuana there. It's pretty good business. A lot of the guys in Casas are mixed up in it. Even some of the big businessmen." He laughed. "There are probably a few that are dragged off into the bushes even now. But it's because of the drugs."

"Don't the cops do anything?"

"Like what?"

"Go and flush them out."

Chet laughed. "There's a lot of rough country up there. You can get lost in those mountains without even trying. The people dealing drugs know the country. The police don't. It's kind of off-limits, a mutual agreement between the cops and

156

the dealers. And there are a few of the cops that are on the take. It's the easy way."

"The mountains are the drug dealers' territory," Randy added, speaking for the first time, "and the police know it. Marijuana is a good cash crop. Even if the police did go up there, they probably wouldn't find much. There are too many places to hide. It would take a regular army to go up there and really clean things out."

"So they never get caught?"

"Not up there," Chet answered. "The hard part for them is getting rid of the stuff once they get it grown. They have to bring it down out of the mountains. That's when the police keep their eyes open. If they haven't been bought off."

We bounced across the flats, taking a longer route I wasn't familiar with. The dirt road wound haphazardly at times, following the smoothest ridges and dropping down into an occasional dip. While Randy and Chet talked and joked, I reverted to silence, thinking once more of home.

Unexpectedly we came upon a rock barricade across the road. It wasn't anything insurmountable, just a dozen or so rocks big enough that you couldn't drive over them.

"Who would throw rocks in the middle of the road out here in the middle of nowhere?" I asked.

"Jake's friends," Chet muttered. "They're just over that way," he said, nodding his head to the west. "The squatters do this all the time. They must have seen us drive out and then come over and blocked the road off."

"For what?" I demanded.

"To keep everybody out. To show everybody that this is their land. Now do you see why my old man wants to run them off?"

"I'm beginning to see," I muttered, lugging the rocks to the side of the road and dumping them.

A couple hundred yards further on we came to a second barricade.

The three of us attacked the rocks and tossed them off

the road. As I turned to return to the truck, I glanced down the road ahead of us. Three Mexicans, a hundred yards or so away, were watching us. As Chet tossed the last rock from the road, the three men each picked up a rock and dropped them into the road, beginning a third barricade.

"They're the ones," Chet exploded. "They're just moving ahead of us. Well, if they think I'm going to be lugging rocks out of the road all the way to Juarez, they're crazy."

Leaving the truck and not bothering to wait for Randy or me, Chet stomped off down the dirt road. The three Mexicans didn't seem concerned by Chet's approach. In fact, they appeared to be inviting a confrontation. As Chet reached the rock barricade, Randy and I climbed into the truck and followed him.

By the time Randy and I pulled up, Chet was speaking in harsh tones to one of the agrarians. Not really wanting to be caught up in the conflict, I stepped to the largest of the seven or eight rocks in the road, picked it up, lugged it to the side of the road, and dropped it on a clump of dry grass. I turned back to get another, this time glancing at the three Mexicans. The oldest of the three might have been in his mid-twenties. One of the others was eighteen or nineteen, and the third looked barely fifteen. Their eyes were dark and defiant.

"Don't do that for them!" Chet snapped. "Let them lug them off. I'm not touching them. I'll show you how the Cramers handle squatters."

I looked again at the three. From a distance they had been annoying antagonists, like pesky flies buzzing about on a sultry afternoon. But up close the three lost their anonymity. They became frustrated and troubled people, just like me.

Gritting his teeth, Chet stepped to the oldest of the three agrarians. The agrarian was fifteen or twenty pounds lighter than Chet, but he was daring Chet to do anything. His black hair dropped down into his eyes, and he brushed it away with dirty fingers.

Pointing to the rocks, Chet barked something in Spanish. The man shook his head.

"He's not going to move them," Randy said nervously. "He's just waiting for us to—"

"*Quita las piedras!*" Chet shouted in the man's face.

The man didn't move but continued to stare at Chet. There was no fear there, just anger and bold defiance.

"I'll wipe that stupid, smug look off your greasy face," Chet muttered in English. "You'll move the rocks."

Chet turned as though he were going to remove the rocks himself, but then came back bringing his fist up and punching the man in the middle. The force of the unexpected blow lifted the man off his feet and knocked him backward where he crumpled into a heap.

The older of the other two Mexicans lunged for Chet, but Chet stepped aside and pushed him away. The agrarian came back, blindly flailing his arms, but he was no fighter. Chet easily blocked his blows and then lashed out twice to his face. Blood gushed from the man's nose.

The youngest agrarian took a couple of steps toward Chet, but Randy grabbed him from behind, pinning his arms and then roughly pushing the kid to the ground. Chet jabbed a finger at the kid and shouted something in Spanish.

"Now we'll see if this other greaser will move these rocks," Chet growled as he returned to the first man, who was still on the ground. Chet grabbed him by the shirt, jerked him to his feet, and pushed him into the road. The man still held his stomach and was unsteady on his feet, but he maintained his balance. "*Quita las piedras!*" Chet yelled, pointing down at the rocks. The man shook his head and glared at him, his eyes blazing with hate. Chet swallowed and threw a wild fist to his face. The man blocked the blow, ducked, and staggered to the side.

"*Quita las piedras!*" Chet wheezed with his fists clenched at his side.

The man came up to his hands and knees, shook his head, and muttered, "No."

Grabbing him by the hair and gripping one arm and twisting

it around behind his back, Chet dragged him to one of the rocks and pushed him onto it. "Pick it up!" he ordered in English. The man shook his head.

I looked on in horror. In a way, I felt detached. This wasn't my fight. And the man had surely brought all this upon himself. But no amount of arguing justified what was happening before me. I thought of the night I had gone to Chet's aid when Julio and his friends attacked him. I had used the excuse that I wanted a fair fight. Deep inside me I knew this was not a fair fight. It was one on one, but not fair. This was all wrong, terribly wrong.

I suddenly felt sick, guilty. "I'll move the lousy rocks," I burst out, stomping forward and grabbing a rock.

"Leave them alone!" Chet challenged, glaring at me. "This little greaser's going to get them."

I glanced at the man at Chet's feet. "He's not going to get anything," I muttered, grabbing another rock.

"Jamison, I want this wimpy weasel to get those rocks."

"And if he doesn't," I asked, "are you going to beat him to death?"

"I'll make him wish he was dead."

"I don't want to wait that long."

"Leave them," Chet shouted, grabbing my arm.

I froze, my eyes locked onto Chet's. For a moment we stared at each other, neither speaking to the other. Gradually Chet's grip on my arm loosened.

"Hey, Chet," Randy rasped, "the other two took off. We've got to get out of here. They'll bring the others back." Randy and I began tossing the rocks from the road while Chet stood next to the man. Slowly the man crawled to the side of the road. He sat down with his legs stretched out in front of him, his body hunched over.

I stared down at the man. Our gazes locked. He had understood none of the English that passed between Chet and me. To him, I was just another one of *them*. In his eyes I was as heartless and cruel as Chet.

I picked up the last rock and tossed it to the side of the road. Chet growled something to the Mexican while Randy tugged on his arm and coaxed him back to the truck. The two of them climbed in. I followed.

"That's how you have to treat them," Chet remarked after we had driven for a few moments in silence. "That's the only thing they understand. They wouldn't even be out there if they knew that was coming."

"Let's forget it," I whispered.

"I was just—"

"Drop it, Cramer!"

Chet glared at me. "What makes you think I've got to listen to you?"

"Because I'm not an agrarian that you can slap around."

"And what's that supposed to mean?"

"If you have any questions," I said, "you stop the truck and I'll show you the difference between me and that agrarian."

"Do you want to walk back to Juarez?"

I looked over at Chet. My eyes cut into him. He turned and looked down the road and continued to drive. We drove most of the way to Juarez in silence. I tried to blot the memory of what had just happened from my mind, but it persisted, lingering like a bad dream. Chet hummed to himself. Randy stared straight ahead, his eyes riveted to the road before him.

"Hey, Hatch, do you want to drive into Casas tonight?" Chet asked as we drove into Juarez. "We could catch a movie and get something to eat. You could go with Tricia. I'll find somebody."

"Sounds all right," Randy agreed, brightening. "You going to take Mag?"

Chet laughed and shook his head. "Naw, she gets too serious."

"You afraid of Julio?" Randy kidded.

"No way. If I wanted to take Mag, I would. And I wouldn't worry about asking Julio."

"If you had an ounce of guts," I muttered, "you'd walk up to her front door and pick her up there."

"I don't want to walk up to her front door."

I stared over at him. "What do you mean?"

"You don't do that down here," he answered sullenly. "At least a Cramer doesn't. That's what Julio has been trying to get me to do."

"Julio *wants* you to ask Mag out?"

"I don't know if he wants me to ask her out, but he figures that if I do take her out I should at least go to the house and pick her up. But Julio Cruz isn't going to tell me how to take a girl out."

"You mean he doesn't care if you date Mag?" I asked, surprised.

Chet shook his head. "Not really."

"So what's stopping you?"

"Are you kidding? If I started dating Mag, my old man would pitch a ragin' fit." Chet shrugged. "He's not big on Mexicans." Chet laughed. "I've got an older brother that pulled that trick on him, and he hasn't gotten over it yet."

"What's wrong with Mag? I mean, she speaks English, she's smart, she's the prettiest girl down here. She's a member of the Church. She's not stuck on herself. I thought you really liked her."

Chet shrugged. "I do, but not for anything serious. I mean, can you see yourself marrying a Mexican?"

I turned away. "So what was the fight about between you and Julio over at the academy?"

"He just told me that if I wanted to see her to go over to the house. Don't worry about it, Jamison. If you lived down here, you'd understand."

"Pull up to the corner," I grumbled. "I can walk from here. I need the fresh air."

"What you so huffy about?" Chet flared, stopping for me to climb out. "What business is Mag of yours, anyway?"

162

"You made her my business when I stepped in to save your bacon from Julio and his two friends."

"Nobody asked you to."

"You should have told me that that night." I stared at Chet. "I thought Mag was something to you. She was something to me. And I only met her once. I liked her. She deserves more than you."

"You let me worry about who I run around with, Jamison."

"I'll do that. But the next time there won't be somebody in the shadows to pull you out."

"I can take care of myself."

"Good. But don't drag Mag around with you in the dark. Because the next time Julio might bring me along. And the next time I won't care if it's a fair fight."

# Chapter Fifteen

It was quiet at supper that evening. Only the steady tinkle of silver on glass broke the silence. Nothing had been said about my absence that day. No one had asked about Mom's call.

"Did you finish the branding?" I asked Grandpa halfway through the meal.

He cleared his throat and reached for the gravy for his potatoes. "It's not exactly a one-man job."

It wasn't an accusation, just a statement, but I felt guilty just the same. "I'm sorry," I muttered. "I just had to—well, to get away for a while. I didn't mean to leave you hanging."

"No problem. I understand."

"Can we do it tomorrow?"

"You up to it?"

"I'm up to it," I said. There was hard determination in my voice. After today all I wanted to do was work until exhaustion erased Mom's devastating news and the memory of the incident on the flats that afternoon.

"I didn't feed the calves," Grandpa remarked.

"I can do it," I quickly volunteered. "I want to do it."

After dinner I made my way to the corral and the calf manger. I broke a couple of bales of alfalfa and dropped them into the manger, filled the box feeder with grain, and then dropped down on a bale of hay.

165

"You going to stay out here all night?" Grandpa asked suddenly. I hadn't heard him approach. He sat down next to me on the bale of hay. We both watched the calves munching their supper. Grandpa pulled a twig of alfalfa from the bale and put it into the corner of his mouth.

For a long time we sat there in silence, listening to the calves munch their alfalfa. Finally Grandpa flipped the twig of alfalfa he had been chewing, wiped his mouth with the back of his hand, and pressed his lips together. "I'm sorry about your folks," he remarked. "I wish things could be different."

"Nothing will ever make it right. Not now."

Grandpa nodded. "Your mother called back. She told us how things were." He cleared his throat. "There's no easy way to break that kind of news to a person."

"Did you know? Before?"

Grandpa reflected for a moment. "Not for sure."

"You didn't ever say."

"There wasn't much to say."

"I guess I should have known." I shook my head. "I always looked forward to coming back from Brazil. I didn't want to come home early or anything like that. But when my mission was over, I was looking forward to going home where two years' absence had made everything so perfect." I smiled and then shook my head.

"There's nothing I wouldn't give away if it would make things right again between your folks. I want you to know that."

I nodded and whispered, "Thanks, Grandpa, but right now I don't want to talk about it. I don't have a dad. Not anymore."

"Don't say that, Jacob."

"I've got to say it. It's the only way I'll make it through this."

"I don't know what's going through your father's mind. I don't know what made him do what he did, but—"

"He didn't even have the guts to call me himself and tell me what was happening. He couldn't even write me a note and say, 'Sorry, kid.' He made Mom do all the dirty work. He traded the whole bunch of us in on that — that whore he's living with."

"Jacob," Grandpa warned, "don't talk like that. No matter what he's done, he's still your father."

"He can do it, but I can't talk about it? You think what he's done is okay?"

"No, he's made his mistakes. But you can't feel like that about him."

"I have a right to feel the way I do."

"It's not a matter of rights. You can't hate just one person. Maybe you start out hating one person. Maybe that's all you want to hate, but soon you find that hate spreading like a cancer. You can't confine it. You either tear it out or it eats away at you and eventually destroys everything you ever loved. Believe me, Jacob, I know."

"You know?" I challenged bitterly. "How could you know? Your father didn't walk out on you."

Grandpa shrugged and nodded his head. "You're right. But I know something about hate."

Grandpa heaved a sigh. "Before you came I wondered how things would work out. It's been good for me to have you here." He smiled. "Thanks, Jacob."

I didn't say anything. I didn't know what to say. I felt a tightness in my throat, and I wanted to say something in return, to tell him how much I appreciated what he had done for me. I suppose at that time I was incapable of saying things like that, but later, when he was gone, I regretted having let the opportunity slip away from me.

"You were right about Julio," I said, groping for something to keep the conversation afloat.

"Julio?"

"Chet and Julio. I guess I shouldn't have been so quick to take Chet's side. How did you know about Chet, about how he felt?"

"I know something about his father."

"Why does he feel that way about Mexicans?"

Grandpa considered the question for a moment. "Years ago people down here didn't have a lot to do with Mexicans. There wasn't a lot of mixing. It was a form of self-preservation."

"A guy wouldn't run around with a Mexican girl then?"

"Never." Grandpa shook his head. "Oh, it happened occasionally, but it was a one-way road to ostracism. People like Calvin Cramer still feel that way."

"Did you ever hear of a Martin Cramer?" I asked, suddenly curious about what Chet had mentioned about his father's uncle.

Grandpa thought for a moment. "Martin Cramer?" He shook his head. "Not that I know of."

"Calvin Cramer's uncle."

"Oh, Martin Sanderson. Yes, I knew him."

"Chet was talking today. About something that—well, something this Martin guy had done." Grandpa studied me without saying anything. "Chet claimed he had killed some men. Nobody ever got him for it. Is it true?"

"Martin claimed it was."

"Do you believe him?"

"I was his bishop for a while, even though he didn't ever have much to do with the Church. I was with him when he died. He claimed then that he had killed some men. There was no reason for him to lie."

"So you think he really got away with it?"

"Got away with it?" Grandpa asked. "He died a shriveled old man, thirty years before his time. His family had left him. He had drunk himself into poverty and early death. I remember when he was young and handsome. He had potential written all over him. Many times I have thought of that young man and the bright future he had. And then I see the shell of the man he was at the end." Grandpa shook his head. "No, Jacob, Martin Sanderson didn't get away with it. He paid for it. More than any of those he dragged off into the brush. And he's still paying."

"What would make a guy do that?"

"Hate. Once you let it in, it spreads like a disease. The only cure is to cut it out."

That evening I took Grandpa's truck and drove over to Laurie's. I didn't want to be alone anymore. Solitude only invited reflection, and I didn't want to think.

"Hey, you in the mood for a ride down to Casas?" I asked Laurie when she came to the door.

"I just had supper," she warned with a laugh. "I couldn't eat any pizza."

I shook my head and smiled. "I'm not in the mood to philosophize, anyway. We could catch a movie."

She took me by the arm and we walked to the truck. We didn't say a lot driving down to Casas, and there wasn't an opportunity to say much in the movie. Afterwards we dropped by a snack bar and each had a cold lemonade while we munched on tortilla chips.

"You're quiet tonight," Laurie commented, staring across the table at me. "What's wrong?"

I tried to smile but failed. "I guess it's just been one of those days."

"I stopped by this afternoon. You weren't there. Martha wasn't sure where you were."

"Did she tell you anything?"

Laurie shook her head.

I chewed on my lower lip. I didn't want to rehash everything again, but I wanted Laurie to know. I felt she needed to know. "Mom and Dad are getting a divorce," I said slowly. I paused a moment and then told her the whole thing, giving details that I had always avoided. Laurie sat and listened, hurting with me.

"I'm sorry," she whispered when I was finished. "I really am sorry, Jacob."

I shrugged. "I guess there's really nothing anybody can do. And today I've wondered if I've come to the point where

169

I don't really care if anything is done or not. Caring only makes you hurt."

"But that's not true, Jacob. You can never stop caring."

I stared down at the tabletop for a moment. When I looked up I was smiling. "There's got to be something more cheerful we could talk about. I've had enough gloom for one day."

"You've convinced me. Let's talk about your plans. Where do you go from Colonia Juarez?"

"I guess my next stop is BYU. I'm going to get into a pre-law program and then go to law school."

"That's a long time."

"One thing I've got a lot of right now is time."

"*Ya es la hora*," called the woman from the counter.

"I guess you just ran out of time. They're going to run us out." Laurie smiled at me as she said it.

It was a quiet ride home. When I walked Laurie to the front door, we paused. I took both her hands and held them as I looked into her face. "Thanks," I whispered. "I needed that tonight." I wet my lips. "You've made it easy for me. Not just tonight. Ever since I got here. I wouldn't have made it without you." I bit down on my lip. "But it's more than that. There's been something different ever since that first morning that we drove to Casas. It's been something I've felt all along. Something I don't ever want to stop feeling."

Laurie leaned into me and nodded her head. "I've felt it too. I was hoping it wasn't something that just I was feeling."

I took her face in my hands and bent over and kissed her softly on the lips. "Thanks, Laurie. Whatever happens, I'm glad that I have you."

# Chapter Sixteen

It was midafternoon when Grandpa and I finished the branding. Grandpa and I had worked up the river all morning and past noon with the smell of burning hair and flesh and dry dust in our nostrils. When the last calf scrambled to its feet, Grandpa straightened up and groaned to himself, slapping at the dirt clinging to his clothes. His face, like mine, was covered with gray dust and streaked with trickles of sweat. He wet his lips and then gazed toward the river where there was a thick stand of tall sycamore trees. "There's a bit of a pool down there," he commented, nodding toward the water and massaging a kink from his back. "I think before we head back I'll wander down and wash some of this dirt off. What I'd really like to do is soak in that river for about a week just to cool off. Working around this fire with the sun bearing down, I feel like I've been broiled and am well done."

I followed Grandpa to the river, where he pulled his shirt off and then dropped to his knees at the edge of the water and began scrubbing the dust from his hands, arms, neck, and face. He moaned contentedly as the water splashed down his back.

I watched him a moment and soon followed his example. Lying on my belly, I plunged my head into the crystal coolness and then pulled it out dripping. The water made my flesh tingle and stiffen, but it was refreshing. I shook my head and sat at the edge of the river, dangling my hands in the water.

Grandpa pushed himself to his feet. As he did, for the first time in my life, I saw the scars. There were two of them, one a long gashing red one just under his ribs on the left side. It pulled and twisted at his white flesh. The second scar was round, purple and concave, a couple inches above and to the left of his heart. The first looked ugly; the second, deadly.

I don't know why the sight of the scars startled me. I knew Grandpa had been shot. Of course, he would have scars. And yet, when I came face to face with the proof of the legend, it stunned me. Suddenly this incident, which had happened years before, burst from its showcase setting where I had always placed it and emerged as a startling reality.

"Do you hate Mexicans?" I asked bluntly.

Grandpa looked down at me. "What was that?" he asked, cocking his head to one side, not sure he had heard me correctly.

I shrugged, looking away. "Do you hate Mexicans?"

Grandpa laughed and squatted down and splashed more water in his face. "I was born in Mexico. My mother was born here. Your mother was born here. Your Uncle Travis's kids are fourth-generation Mexicans."

"But you're not one of them," I stated, sweeping my hand along the surface of the water and sending up a crystal spray.

"Oh, I might be a little more bleached than the average Mexican, but I'm Mexican all right. Mexico's the only home I've got. The only home I've ever had."

Nodding to his scars, I remarked, "Those prove that to the Mexicans you're just another gringo. Don't you hate Mexicans for that?"

Grandpa studied his scars as though he had just discovered them. Slowly he put his shirt on. "That was a long time ago, Jacob. I hardly remember it anymore. It's funny how you can forget something like that. I remember the time when I could think of nothing else. But fifty years can change a lot of memories." He smiled as he buttoned his shirt and stuffed the tail into his pants. "I'm not even sure who did this. And the older

172

I get, the less I care. It really doesn't matter now. I don't need to drag it around with me like a ball and chain."

"Is it over?" I challenged. "Those squatters out on Shupe land don't think it's over. They'd do the same thing today if you gave them the chance."

"It can be over for me."

"You've forgotten about it, just like that?"

"You have to learn to forget things like that."

"Did you always turn the other cheek?"

Grandpa stared into the water. The traces of a smile pulled at his lips as he stepped to a rock and sank upon it. "Not back then." He pursed his lips. "You know, Jacob, it's been fifty years this past spring," he mused. "Fifty years." He shook his head. "That's a long time. A guy doesn't forget something like that."

He cupped his hands together, scooped up some water, and let it trickle back into the river. "You didn't know Harold. A person really can't understand unless he knew Harold." Grandpa rubbed the back of his neck with a wet hand. "Harold was one of those guys that — " He shook his head. "Well, once or twice in a lifetime you meet someone like Harold. He was three years older than I and something of a hero for me. Everybody loved him. He was about to marry Millie Romney, a girl from down here."

Grandpa pondered a moment, his mind traveling back in time. "Harold was before his time. Back then whites and Mexicans didn't mix. We didn't mind Mexicans working for us. The men didn't mind being friendly with the Mexican men. But we sure didn't want them talking to our sisters or going to our dances and socials. Harold didn't feel that way. He wanted to preach the gospel to them. I don't mean running off to Mexico City or the far corners of the country like other folks. He wanted to do the preaching right here in Colonia Juarez. He was the greatest champion of Mexican-Anglo relations that happened along." Grandpa's jaw clamped tight. "And for all that," he went on bitterly, "he was gunned down by a bunch of Mexicans who didn't know him at all. There were a dozen Anglos those Mexicans could have shot for just cause. But no, they had to shoot the one man who was their genuine champion, and they didn't even know it."

"How did it happen?"

"Oh, it was about like now. We were having trouble with our land. There was a group of Mexicans on the south end of our range giving us some problems. We figured they'd stolen some of our cattle, torn down some of our fences. There were those who wanted to ride down there and clean the whole bunch of them out. Dad and Harold talked peace, though." Grandpa shook his head. "I was with the others. I was for driving them out.

"One day Harold and I rode out that way and caught these people right in the act. They'd butchered one steer and were ready to start on the other one when we rode up. Harold was cool about the whole thing. He was willing to give them the butchered steer, but he figured he'd take the other one. Not me, I wanted to get every last one of those responsible."

"Did you know any of them?" I asked.

Grandpa shook his head. "And I wasn't paying any attention to them anyway. All I could see was that gutted calf. I'm not sure what happened. Harold climbed off his horse to get the other steer, and someone shot him."

"You mean they just gunned him down?"

"He was dead before he hit the ground. I jumped off my horse to help Harold and I took two slugs before I reached him."

"Who found you?"

"Nobody. I suffered there most of the afternoon, fighting off thirst and pain the whole time. I was in and out of consciousness."

"What happened to the Mexicans?"

"They left. Just walked away. And there I was within sight of their homes. I could hear them in their village nearby. And there was a stream close by. I could hear the water. It tormented me all afternoon."

"And no one came to help you?"

"Someone came. I saw his feet, but I didn't know who it was and he didn't help me. I knew I was going to die. There was no question in my mind. I was just waiting for it to happen.

"Then my horse came back. It was strange. I opened my eyes and there she was. I don't know how I ever made it into the saddle, but I did. I passed out, but the horse took me home. When I finally came to, Harold had been buried for a couple of days."

For several minutes Grandpa and I sat staring into the river. I picked up a pebble and tossed it into the water and watched the ripples spread outward. "And nobody tried to catch the ones who did it?"

"Not really."

"You mean, they got away?"

"There were no clues. I couldn't tell them anything."

"But what about all those people who lived there? You said you could see their homes."

"When the officials questioned them, they played ignorant. And the officials didn't push them. It wasn't a big thing to them that a gringo had been killed."

"Did you ever want revenge?"

Grandpa looked out across the narrow river. A humorless smile played upon his lips, and he nodded his head. "Before that, I had been indifferent to Mexicans. At best I had endured them. But after Harold's death I hated them. I wanted revenge in the worst way. As I struggled to recover, I made a vow. I promised myself that someday I would make them pay for what they had done. They would remember Jacob Martineau. I would never let them forget. If I never did another thing in my life, those people would suffer."

"And did you ever get your revenge?"

He shook his head. "Years later I discovered I was following a dead-end path. I gave up on it."

175

"You never went back to those people?"

"Back?"

"To the village near where you almost died."

Grandpa stared at me for a moment as though not under-standing the question. "Of course, I went back. Many times."

"Where is it?"

"San Diego."

"San Diego?" I gasped, my eyes narrowing in disbelief. "Not your San Diego?"

"I thought you knew."

"Knew? How could I know?" I pushed myself to my feet. Suddenly I felt betrayed. It was as though Grandpa had just played a cruel joke on me. None of this made sense. I didn't want the village to be San Diego. That made everything so— so incomprehensible, so wrong. "But that's where your branch is," I stammered. "Why would you—" I couldn't bring myself to ask the question. I didn't want to hear the answer, and Grandpa didn't say anymore about it that day.

# Chapter Seventeen

When we drove into the yard that evening, Uncle Travis and Calvin Cramer were there waiting for us. Their faces were a picture of gloom. Grandpa nodded a silent greeting to both of them as he stepped from the truck.

"Bad news, Dad," Uncle Travis spoke gravely.

Grandpa waited without commenting.

"There's another camp of agrarians over on Spilsbury's ranch."

Grandpa looked from Uncle Travis to Calvin Cramer and then back to Uncle Travis. "Spilsbury's a long ways from Shupe's place." Uncle Travis nodded. "When?"

Uncle Travis shrugged. "At least three or four days. Spilsbury hadn't been out that way for several days."

Grandpa turned and grabbed the branding irons from the back of the truck, carried them into the barn, and returned a moment later. "How many are out on Spilsbury's place?"

"It's a smaller group," Uncle Travis answered. "A dozen, maybe a few more."

"Does this change anything?"

"I think so," Calvin answered.

"That means we take the law into our own hands?"

"There is no law out there. Not until we make one." Calvin tore his hat from his head. "Jake, we've got to move or we're going to be standing around empty-handed with dumb looks on our faces. If we wait, some of us aren't going to have a ranch."

"Just because there are two camps doesn't mean we have to charge off and do something crazy."

"Dad, there are three camps. Calvin saw another one this afternoon."

Grandpa looked over at Calvin. Calvin stared back for a moment and then slowly shook his head. "On your place, Jake. To the west of Cuautemoch and San Diego. Not far from the road that goes to the mountains."

Grandpa's eyes narrowed. He thought for a moment and then smiled. "But there's nothing out there. Why would anyone set up camp there?"

"Why would they do a lot of things? I don't know, but they're on your place now."

"It doesn't make sense. There's not even water out there."

"There's that little bunch of trees to the west."

"Trees?" Grandpa countered, grinning. "I might call them bushes. I'm not sure I'd go so far as to call them trees."

"Whatever," Uncle Travis shrugged. "But there's a little spring there."

Grandpa laughed. "There's not enough water in that spring to give a thirsty horse a drink twice a day. There's not enough there to water a field. Or even a garden."

"There might be if they put a well in," Calvin pointed out. "There's water there if they bring it up."

"I'd hate to gamble on how much water is there. And those people don't have money to put in a well."

"You're missing the point, Jake. Maybe it's not the agrarians we even have to worry about."

"How do you figure?"

"Maybe there are others behind these agrarians, others that want more than just a little corner of our ranch. They're stirring up the agrarians to push us right out of Colonia Juarez, clear out of Mexico. And then the real organizers, the ones backing these agrarians, will move in and sit down to the whole dish of pie and they'll drop a few crumbs to the agrarians to keep them happy."

"That's some pretty wild speculation, Calvin."

"Maybe, but your camp looks different. I saw only one woman. No kids. They're not even camped by the spring. Their camp's out toward that little promontory north of there."

"The promontory?" Grandpa laughed. "They're not agrarians then. They're fools. If they put their field or garden there, how are they ever going to water it? Even with a well."

"I can't figure them out, Dad. When Calvin told me about them, I rode out with José Luís and had a look. This is a different breed. They're not ragged-looking like the others. They just look like they're waiting around, taking their time, trying to prove a point. And they don't look like the type you could push around."

"How many are there?"

"Half a dozen or so."

For a long time Grandpa stood with his hands stuffed in his rear pockets and kicked at the gravel with the toe of his boot. Slowly he shook his head. "It doesn't make sense."

"To me, none of it makes sense," Calvin interjected. "Why any of them would move out on any part of this range is beyond me. But they do it."

"Tomorrow I'll ride out and take a look."

"And then what?"

"I'll see what Alvarez says."

"Alvarez," Calvin muttered. "Alvarez is in Chihuahua City. It's not his ranch on the chopping block. He doesn't care. We're wasting our breath with him."

"He moved them the last time when they were out on Whettens' place."

Calvin glared. "Suit yourself, Jake. If you need my help, you know where you can find me."

"I had a good talk with Carlos Alvarez. He's on our side. He thinks he can have those squatters moved before the end of the month."

"He thinks."

"He gave me his word."

"His word?" Calvin scoffed. "And what kind of *mordida* did the honorable Carlos Alvarez accept for his word?"

"Alvarez said he'd use troops again if he had to. We can wait until the end of the month."

"Can we? Have you heard the rumors from Paquimé? I have it from a good source that the workers are just waiting for the apples to come on. As soon as the apples are ripe, they're going to strike. And not just the workers at Paquimé. We might have trouble finding pickers. With ripe apples on the trees, they're going to have the upper hand."

"Mexico is full of people looking for work."

"Not if the old workers won't let them in."

"The state police will be there."

"The first apples will be ready for picking in about a month, the same time Alvarez has promised the troops. But if things blow up down at Paquimé and in the orchards, nobody's going to worry about a few squatters up here. Stop kidding yourself, Jake. Things aren't good. And they're getting worse."

The next day Grandpa left early and drove out to see the squatters' camp. He didn't return for lunch. It was almost dusk when he finally pulled into the yard. Uncle Travis and I were there waiting for him.

"Well, what did you find out?" Uncle Travis asked as Grandpa stepped from the truck.

Grandpa leaned his forearms on the hood of the truck and stared out toward the corrals. "I talked to José Luís. He found out a few things. That group has been in the area the last three or four days, a couple days before they settled on our land. As far as farming goes, it's a lousy piece of ground. If they're just trying to prove a point, they chose the right piece of land for it. Who's going to bother them out there?"

"José Luís doesn't think they're a problem?"

"He doesn't know. They look —" Grandpa shook his head. "There's something different about them. And I can't put my finger on it. They want to look like agrarians, but I get this gut feeling that that's all a front."

"Do you think this agrarian thing is more organized than we think, like Calvin said?"

Grandpa chuckled. "I wish I knew, Travis. But there's one thing I'm convinced of. When we do move, we better make sure we've got some backing."

"Meaning Alvarez?"

"I wish I had more faith in Carlos."

Uncle Travis stared at Grandpa. "You mean you don't?"

"Carlos has stepped on too many toes the last few years. He knows it. He doesn't want to do anything stupid politically. On the other hand, he would like to do something that would be impressive. If he can do that and help us too, he will. But he sees the risks. The day it's to his advantage to move the agrarians, he'll be ready. If it's to his advantage to let them stay, then he won't bother them."

"I thought he was a friend of yours."

"He's got to survive, too."

Grandpa pulled a toothpick from his shirt pocket and dug at one of his back teeth. "Do you remember a Pepe Carranza?"

Uncle Travis thought for a moment. "Carranza. There are a few Carranzas around. Pepe. Pepe. Wasn't there a Pepe Carranza that worked for Whettens a while back? Yeah. And he got caught stealing diesel fuel. They figured he'd been walking off with tools and things, too. The Whettens ran him off. Is that the one?"

"Probably."

"The last I heard he was working for Walt Shupe. Then he pulled some of the same kind of stuff."

Grandpa chewed on his toothpick and then flipped it toward the barn. "That's the one."

"Why you interested in Pepe Carranza?"

"Somebody found him this morning between here and Chupi. Dead."

"How?"

"Neck was broken."

"An accident?"

"Somebody wanted it to look that way."

"What would he be doing up in the mountains? He doesn't have a family there, does he?"

Grandpa shrugged.

"Are the police involved?"

"They say it's accidental."

"You don't think it was accidental?"

"José Luís doesn't think so."

"Why?"

"Gut feeling maybe."

"No other reason?"

"He doesn't think he died in the mountains. Two days ago Pepe was running around with this group that's on our place."

"I don't think Pepe's involved with the agrarians," Uncle Travis objected. "He's a common thief. He's not interested in land. Not unless there's easy money."

"Maybe you're right."

"Are you worried?"

Grandpa thought for a long time. He seemed somber. Finally he nodded his head. "Yes, Travis, I'm worried. I'll laugh for Calvin Cramer, but my insides are all tied in knots."

# Chapter Eighteen

Sunday morning I decided to sleep in. I even considered staying home from church. Just this once, I told myself. I didn't want to go to church and hear all the stuff about forever families.

I was still in bed, suspended between sleep and drowsiness, when there was a knock at the door. My eyes opened and blinked at the clock on the dresser—8:45 A.M. I rolled over and closed my eyes. There was another knock, this one heavier. I pushed up on my elbow and mumbled, "Yeah."

"Can I come in for a minute?" Grandpa called to me.

I hesitated, then tossed off the sheet, swung out of bed, grabbed my pants, and pulled them on. "Come in," I mumbled as I buttoned and zipped my pants.

The knob turned and the door swung open. For a moment Grandpa stood in the doorway. He was dressed in his Sunday suit and his dress boots. Scratching the back of his neck, he finally stepped into the room. He was ill at ease. He strolled to the window, pulled back the curtains, and peered out. Bright streams of sunshine poured past him into the room. I blinked and squinted at the glare and dropped down on the edge of the bed.

"I was going to San Diego in a few minutes," he said, looking out the window. "It's been a few weeks since I visited."

I didn't respond.

"I was wondering if you would go with me," he said, turning to face me.

"I'd rather not," I replied, standing up and snatching my shirt from the back of the chair.

"I thought you liked San Diego."

I shrugged. "I guess once is enough. There's not much to see."

"Because of what happened there fifty years ago?"

I stepped to the dresser and rummaged through my after-shave bottles, brush, wallet, and other things strewn about. With my back to Grandpa I swallowed and chewed on my lower lip. "Maybe that has something to do with it. I don't know. So many things have happened the last little while."

"I was about your age—a few years younger—when the world shattered in my hands."

"I'm not sure that what happened to you is the same thing that's happened to me."

"I lost a brother."

"I lost a whole family," I whispered hoarsely. "And when I think of that," I swallowed, "I get a hard knot in the pit of my stomach. I want Dad to hurt, like the rest of us are hurting."

"And then what?"

I turned and faced Grandpa, taken back. "What do you mean, and then what?"

"After you make him hurt, then what?"

"Then, well, then I will have done what I wanted to do," I stammered. I looked away and stepped to the window, brushing at a fly that was trying to escape through the screen.

"You don't know what it's like to look back fifty years, do you?" I turned and faced Grandpa. He shook his head. "Before you are forced to look back with hate still festering in your craw, I'd like you to see and feel something else. There is something else, you know."

Grandpa and I didn't speak much as we traveled over the rutted road to San Diego. We were a little late in arriving at the *casa de oración*. The members were just getting ready to begin their meeting when we walked in. Everything stopped, and amid shouts of *"hermano"* Grandpa and I were pulled into the room while people pumped our hands and gave us uninhibited *abrazos*.

Not even my aloofness could combat the warmth of the welcome, and I soon found myself smiling and feeling a bit of the magic I had experienced during my first visit several weeks earlier. I didn't know these people. They didn't know me. But because I was with Grandpa, I was entitled to all they had to offer. I, too, was a guest.

I sat through the meetings, understanding little and saying nothing, but I took in everything, intrigued by this strange place and its peculiar people.

When the meeting ended, each person approached Grandpa and me before leaving, shook our hands, offered us their homes and their simple Sunday meals, and invited us back. It was almost ritual. Grandpa graciously declined each invitation and soon we were the only ones left. Grandpa had promised José Luís that he would lock the doors before leaving. The two of us remained in the small, quaint chapel amid the metal folding chairs and the lingering warmth of the people. Grandpa stood at one of the windows looking out. I sat in a chair leaning forward with my forearms on my knees, staring at the wooden floor.

After several minutes of silence, Grandpa turned from the window and strolled to the front of the chapel and leaned against the rough pulpit. "You know, Jacob, I never tire of coming to San Diego."

I sat up and leaned back in my chair.

Grandpa paced back and forth for a moment in front of the pulpit. "You know, I could go to any family in San Diego, member or nonmember, it would make no difference, and I could ask for anything. If it was within their power to give it to me, they would." Grandpa looked out the window and pointed. "And yet, fifty years ago, not a hundred yards from where you and I are right now, just the other side of the stream,

I lay out there dying, and the people of San Diego wouldn't raise a finger to help me. I was dying and choking from thirst. They wouldn't bring me a cup of water. They would have done more for a stray dog." He heaved a sigh and leaned against the window sill. "Doesn't that make you wonder what happened in those fifty years?"

He moved from the window and sat down in a chair in the front row. "For several years I didn't step foot in San Diego, but I always thought of ways to settle the score. I finally decided that if I could buy enough of the land around San Diego, I could choke this place and strangle it into oblivion. I don't know if it would have even worked, but that's what I tried to do. I even bought up some of the land around here."

Grandpa was quiet a moment. He brushed at some dust on his pants with the back of his hand. "I don't remember how Martha found out. It wasn't something we discussed. She knew what had happened in San Diego. She was frightened by the place and never came here, but when I finally explained what I wanted to do, she was horrified. That was when she gave me her ultimatum: I could have my hate for San Diego or my love for her. But I couldn't have them both."

Grandpa pressed his lips together and stared intently at the floor. For several minutes he was quiet. I wondered if that was the end of the story. When he spoke again, he had changed subjects entirely.

"When I was growing up, there was a boy named Arnold Gates. He was two years older than I, but a little slow. The rest of us kids teased Arnold unmercifully. He wanted so much to be one of us, and we wouldn't let him. We made him do our dirty work. And he would because he was desperate to please us."

Grandpa took a deep breath, pushed himself from the chair, and walked to the window and gazed out. "When I was just thirteen, a group of us were going on a camping trip. We were going to ride our horses up the river and spend the night. Arnold happened along as we were packing our things and begged us to let him come along. We told him we'd consider it if he'd help us out. He was more than willing, and we put him to work doing every little odd job we could find. We loaded him down with packs and bedrolls. He helped us put our packs on our horses. He slaved for us until his tongue was hanging out.

"Finally when we were all ready, we sent him home to get his own things, and then we left him. We laughed all the way up the river, because we'd tricked old Arnold Gates, stupid old Arnold Gates."

Grandpa sucked in a breath of air and continued gazing out the window. "They found Arnold Gates the next morning in Fritz Romney's barn. Dead! Hanging from the rafters. All night while we were up the river, laughing and having a good time, Arnold was hanging in that barn. His folks hadn't looked for him. They thought he was with us. So when no one was looking, when no one seemed to care, Arnold had climbed into the loft, put the rope around his neck, and jumped.

"Not many days go by that I don't think of Arnold. I wasn't in the barn when Arnold hung himself. But I can't help thinking that we all helped push him out of that loft."

Grandpa shook his head. "I don't know if I could have prevented Arnold's death. Maybe had he not jumped that day he would have jumped another. I don't know. But I could have changed his life. I'm sure of it. I could have made his life, as difficult as it was, a little better. Jacob, you don't know how many times I've dreamed myself into that barn just before Arnold made his leap. And every time I've stopped him. But they were just empty dreams."

He turned from the window and faced me. There were tears in his eyes. I had never imagined Grandpa capable of tears. He pulled a handkerchief from his back pocket, blew his nose, and dabbed roughly at his eyes. Then he walked from the window and paced the floor in front of the pulpit again. And as he paced, he spoke. "I met José Luís years ago, several years after I had married Martha. I hired him for a week thinning apples. He was a good worker so I kept him on longer. Soon he was permanent.

"I had never had a friend like him. I enjoyed working with him more than anyone else — even though he was Mexican, and at that time I distrusted most Mexicans.

"One day José Luís and I were working up the river. It had been hot and we decided to go for a swim." Grandpa chuckled, remembering. "Here we were, two grown men, and in the middle of the afternoon we decided to go swimming. I was in the water splashing about when I noticed him staring at me, at my scars. Casually I remarked that I had been shot in San Diego years before. With his eyes riveted to those old wounds, his eyes filled with tears. I didn't know what to say. It was all so crazy. He kept babbling in Spanish, 'You're alive. You're alive.' "

"Was he there?" I asked.

Grandpa nodded.

"And you had never suspected?"

"There was no reason to. When I first met him he had only recently moved from Durango."

"So how was he there?"

"A few days before Harold and I were shot, he had gone to visit an uncle in San Diego. He was there when the men killed the steer. Then he remembered two gringos riding up. Everything happened so quickly. The shots were fired and two men were lying on the ground.

"After that everyone just went away. No one wanted to be there. No one wanted to be reminded of what had happened. It was as though they thought that if they went back to their homes and their work, it would all be forgotten."

"Did he know who had done it?" I asked, suddenly consumed with curiosity.

Grandpa shook his head. "It happened so quickly, and José Luís didn't know the people. He didn't notice who fired the guns. About all he could remember clearly was running away.

"Later he went back. He could see that Harold was dead,

but he noticed that I was still breathing. He saw me open my eyes and heard me groan and ask for water, but he was afraid to help. And so he ran away again, but he knew I would die very soon. He ran and ran until he was exhausted. It was while he was out there trying to escape that he found my horse. He caught her and led her back to where I was. When he came back later, it was almost dark and I was gone. Shortly after that he returned to Durango.

"For the next ten or twelve years he stayed in Durango, but he could never erase the incident from his memory. At night he would dream. The dream was always the same. I would be lying in a pool of blood, begging him to save me. He would try to move to help me but he was paralyzed. He wanted to turn away but couldn't. Always he was made to watch helplessly as my life oozed out of me and I became silent and still. Only when I was dead was he able to move and then he would wake up.

"He felt no guilt where Harold was concerned. There was nothing he could have done for him. But he was responsible for my death. He carried that guilt around with him. When he returned to San Diego and Colonia Juarez, he never talked about the incident. No one else mentioned it. It was as though people had shut it away in their mind's closet, closed the door, determined never to open it.

"And then he saw me in the river and realized for the first time in almost fifteen years that the man he had allowed to die was still very much alive, was right before him. That day up the river José Luís came face to face with his Arnold Gates. And he was alive!"

"Did you ever ask José Luís who had been there?" I questioned.

"I found out that it didn't matter."

"It didn't matter?"

"All those years I had believed that no one in San Diego had really cared about what happened to Harold and me. And then along came José Luís, who years later wept for joy because

I was alive. In his mind a nameless gringo had died fifteen years earlier; then a friend was resurrected in that stranger's place. I struggled with anger, with my desire for revenge. But eventually that new person, that person that José Luís had resurrected, won out. In everybody else's mind two gringos had died that day. I decided to leave it that way. I would bury my hate. It took weeks, months, even years."

"So the people in San Diego don't know?"

"They aren't the same people. Perhaps some of them were there that day. Some have heard versions of the story, but that's all it is to them — a story. I would guess that few if any realize I was one of those gringos. But it doesn't matter."

Grandpa was silent. Then a smile tugged at his lips. "You know, Jacob, it's strange how things happen. José Luís was always afraid that he had let me die; instead, he saved my life. Not because he brought me my horse, but because of what he said and did while we were up the river."

"You baptized him after that?"

Grandpa nodded.

"But it seems unfair."

"Unfair?"

"There was no justice. Someone should pay for what was done. Not José Luís. He was innocent. But someone fired those shots. Someone killed Harold. And almost killed you. They should pay."

"I wonder what I'll think when I come face to face with Arnold Gates. I wonder if I'll insist on strict justice?" He breathed deeply and shook his head. "I will never have the opportunity to change what happened to Arnold Gates, but I can still change what happens to San Diego. I never want to go back and be the person I was before José Luís found me. I never want to resurrect that other gringo in me."

Grandpa smiled. "You know, Jacob, I was always angry because Harold died. I was angry that Harold with all his goodness, compassion, and kindness had been snuffed out." Grandpa shook his head. "Harold lives in San Diego. All he ever wanted still lives here. The only things that have died are bits and pieces of prejudice and hate. And I carried those. So in the end I find that I died and Harold lived.

"I told you once that I had made a vow. I wanted the people of San Diego to remember Jacob Martineau." He chuckled. "They remember, Jacob. They remember."

For a long time neither of us spoke. We just stood up and walked slowly from the *casa de oración*. We locked the door behind us, walked down the narrow gravel path across the bridge, and climbed into the truck.

"It's different with me, you know," I commented, as Grandpa started the engine.

"How's that?"

I turned to him. "What happened here was — well, an accident. They were strangers. You were left by people who didn't care for you in the least, who had no reason to care for you. I have no Arnold Gates in my past."

"But you have a father in your present. And before you know it, you'll be looking back."

# Chapter Nineteen

"You do know where you're going, don't you?" Laurie kidded as we rode our horses across the flats west of Cuautemoch and San Diego Monday afternoon.

"You said you wanted to go for a ride," I grinned over at her.

"Can't you go for a ride and still know where you're going?" she continued to tease. "I hope you don't drag us both out here and get us lost. And I think I'm getting saddle sore."

"And here I thought you were a regular cowgirl."

"Just because I was raised in Colonia Juarez doesn't mean I go around roping bulls and branding calves. I'll bet you'd really be impressed if you had to ride out here with some girl with calluses on her hands, burrs in her hair, and manure on her boots."

I laughed. "Settle down, girl. I'm just letting my horse take me where he wants. You ready for a rest?"

"Two hours ago."

"Let's see what's on that rise over there."

We rode toward the rise, picking our way through the desert grass and brush. Laurie shielded her eyes against the sun's glare with her forearm as the horses plodded along. I was glad that I had asked her to come. At first I'd considered riding out on my own, just to clear my thoughts. After my visit with Grandpa the day before, my mind was a scramble.

When we reached the rise, we discovered that it was more than just a hill but a rather large plateau or promontory. On the far side, which was about a quarter of a mile away, an area had been cleared off. Just off the promontory were three make-shift tents.

"Hey, this is that third squatter's camp, I'll bet," I remarked, squinting across the top of the promontory. "They're clearing the land down there on the other end."

"The agrarians?" Laurie questioned, looking down toward the camp and then back at me.

"It's got to be. Let's ride over that way."

"Jacob," Laurie called out, "I don't think we should. I don't trust them. Remember what happened to Clyde Shupe?"

"I'm not planning to sabotage their well. I'm just going to ride by, not invite ourselves to dinner."

Laurie was reluctant, but she followed.

"They've even cleared over on this side," I observed as we rode along, taking our time. The ground had been smoothed some, rocks removed, brush and clumps of grass dug up. But the brush had been left in place. "Strange field," I muttered. "It's almost like they don't want anyone to know that they've been clearing things on this end. It's pretty narrow down this way, too."

"Are they planning to grow anything up here?" Laurie asked.

"Seems like it. But I don't see how they can. Grandpa was right. These jokers can't be farmers, just fools. They'd never water this land up here. I'm no farmer, but even I can see that."

We reached the far side of the plateau and looked down on the camp. It was deserted. A half mile from the camp a dirt road passed.

"Where does that road go?"

"To the mountains. If you want to go to Colonia García or Chupi, you take that road."

"This is the squatter camp, all right."

"Let's get out of here, Jacob. This place gives me the creeps."

I laughed. "Oh, don't worry. Nobody's around. And we're not hurting anything."

"But I don't want them finding us here."

"Finding us here? This is Grandpa's land."

"Jacob, please."

I shook my head. "All right. There should be a spring around here someplace." I looked around. To the west was a slight dip filled with mesquite brush and a few straggly trees. It was the only real green spot close by.

"That must be it," I said, pointing. "Let's ride over and give the horses a drink before heading back." I glanced back once before riding off the promontory and noticed what a strange field these agrarians were making. They were clearing the land but making no effort to till it.

The spring was situated in a small stand of mesquite and brush. There was a bit of grass. None of the trees was large enough to throw a great deal of shade; but after being out in the hot sun, anything was refreshing. We found the spring, a mere trickle that bubbled out from some rocks and gravel and formed a small pool and then trickled off among the mesquite and eventually disappeared again in the dry ground. Several cattle trails cut through the brush to the edge of the small pool.

Laurie and I both took a long drink and then let the horses take their turn at the pool's edge while we sat back under a straggly tree, the largest in the whole grove. It felt good to be out of the saddle and the sun and able to just stretch out with our backs to the tree and relax. The only sounds were the buzz of bugs and the gurgle of water.

I took Laurie's hand and held it in both of mine as I watched the two horses fight against their bits to munch at the few strands of grass that grew along the edge of the pool.

"It's hard to believe that the summer is more than half over," Laurie sighed. She laughed softly and looked up at me.

"When I left BYU and came home, I thought the summer would drag by." She smiled. "It hasn't. It's moved so fast. Now I don't want it to end. I'd like it to be summer in Colonia Juarez forever."

I put my arm around her, pulled her close, and touched my lips to her forehead. I wanted to hold her like that without ever letting her go.

"When you leave here at the end of the summer," she whispered, "will I see you again?"

"You won't be able to keep me away," I said, laughing softly. "We'll both be at BYU." I shook my head. "I won't stay away. I can promise you that."

Laurie pondered for a moment. "You know," she remarked slowly, "I didn't think I would ever meet someone I could really like in Colonia Juarez. I didn't ever consider looking. It's strange that it was here that I met you. You've never been in Colonia Juarez in the winter, have you?" she asked, changing the subject. "You'll have to come for Christmas."

"Someone will have to invite me first."

"Consider it done."

"I accept. And don't ever think for a second that I will let you back out of that invitation."

"Will your family give you up for a Christmas?"

"By Christmas, it probably won't make any difference."

For a long while we were quiet, and a bit of the gloom I had felt the last few days came back. It seemed that I would always have to live with that gloom.

"I think you ought to go back home," Laurie whispered. "I don't want to see you leave Juarez, but you'll always feel something is unfinished if you don't go back."

I looked over at her and took her hand. "Maybe I just need someone to go with me." I pulled her close and kissed her softly on the lips.

"Maybe all you have to do is ask."

"We'd better be getting back," I mumbled, pushing myself to my feet and reaching down and pulling Laurie up.

As we led our horses from the grove, I spotted something back in the mesquite, a gray canvas tarp that blended into the vegetation. "I wonder what that is," I muttered half to myself, handing my horse's reins to Laurie and pushing off the trail into the bushes toward the tarp.

"Do you think you should?" Laurie called after me. "Maybe it belongs to the agrarians."

"I've got a right to at least look," I called back over my shoulder. "After all, this is still Grandpa's land. Maybe this tarp is Grandpa's."

I reached the tarp and threw back one of the corners. There was a stack of odd-looking bales.

"It's just hay," Laurie said at my elbow. She had followed me. "Why would Jake leave hay out here?"

"Pretty lousy looking hay if you ask me," I muttered. "I've never seen hay baled quite like this. Grandpa doesn't bale hay like this. I wonder — "

The grumble of an engine sounded from the distance and stopped me in midsentence. Laurie tugged at my arm. "Come on, Jacob, let's go. I don't want anybody thinking we're snooping around. Even if this is Jake's land."

I was about to drop the tarp over the bales when I caught a strange odor. I sniffed, wrinkled my nose. Cautiously I reached out and pulled a few strands of the green dried plants from one of the bales. I studied them for a moment and held them to my nose.

Suddenly a cold, clutching fear reached into my middle. My breath was sucked away and the blood drained from my face as I turned to Laurie. "That's not Grandpa's," I rasped. "And it's not hay." I looked about. I knew we had been alone, but suddenly I was worried that someone would find us here.

"What's the matter?" Laurie asked, seeing the worry on my face.

I reached out and took Laurie's hand and began pulling her back to the horses, letting the tarp fall over the bales. "Let's get out of here!"

"What's the matter, Jacob?" She tried to smile, but the smile was uncertain. "Are you just trying to scare me? What's the matter?"

"That's marijuana."

"Oh, come on, Jacob," she protested.

"I've never seen it like that. But that's what it is. I'm positive."

"But why —" She swallowed and glanced back at the tarp. "What's it doing here?"

"I don't know."

"And if that's what it is, where would it come from? I mean —"

"Chet was saying they grow the stuff in the mountains. Is that true?"

"Well, I guess. But this isn't the mountains. And why would they bring it down here and just leave it?"

I shook my head. "I don't know. None of this makes sense. But we've got to get out of here and let Grandpa know."

"Are you sure, Jacob?"

I nodded.

"But why would they put it here, so close to the agrarian camp? Wouldn't they be afraid that the agrarians would find it and —"

"The agrarians!" I exclaimed, cutting her off. "That's why the camp's here." I grabbed her hand and squeezed. I wasn't aware how hard I held her until she winced and pulled away. "They're not agrarians anymore than you or I."

"But —"

"That's why this camp is so different. They're moving drugs."

"I don't understand."

"Somebody brings the stuff out of the mountains. Maybe these guys. They hold it until they can get rid of it."

"But why here? It doesn't make sense. Why leave it here in the middle of nowhere with no way to get rid of it?"

"The field, Laurie. The field." Suddenly everything was

very clear. "No wonder they don't care if they can't get water up on that promontory. They're not planting anything. That's a runway. For a small plane. There's probably not a decent place in the mountains to land their plane, so they land it out here. Everybody thinks they're agrarians like the others, but all the while they're shipping marijuana out of the mountains."

"Are you sure?"

"I'm not sure of anything except that we need to get out of here."

I pushed back to the horses, pulling Laurie behind me. I was about to take the horses out the way we'd come in. "Wait," I cautioned, stopping and holding up my hand. "We've got to go out the back way. We can't go past that camp. Not now."

"But Colonia Juarez is back the other way," Laurie protested, pointing in the direction of the camp. "We've got to go that way."

I stopped, my mind a jumble of thoughts and fears. "Where's San Diego from here?" I asked. She pointed to the southeast, away from Colonia Juarez. "How far?"

"Maybe a couple of miles. Maybe more. I don't know, Jacob. What are we going to do?"

"For a start, we're getting out of here." I pointed back to the tarp. "There's at least a half ton of marijuana there. That's a lot of pesos. That's a lot of dollars. Whoever belongs to that stuff doesn't want anybody snooping around."

Laurie's face was chalky; her lips were like thin, tight lines across her face. She stared in wide-eyed silence. "Mount up. We've got to put as much distance between us and this place as we can."

Leaving from the far side of the grove, we headed toward San Diego, first at a fast walk, then a trot, and finally a full gallop. Once in San Diego we took the main road back to Colonia Juarez.

The horses were lathered and ready to drop when we finally rode into the yard. Grandpa was in the barn working when we rode up and jumped from our saddles.

"You trying to kill those animals?" he asked, coming from the barn. "You ride a horse like that in the heat of the day, and he'll drop."

"Grandpa," I gasped, gulping and wetting my lips, "that camp out on your place, it's not an agrarian camp. They're moving drugs."

Twenty minutes later I had finished the story. Grandpa was quiet for a moment. "You're sure that's what it was?" he asked me for at least the tenth time.

"I'm positive, Grandpa. I know."

He nodded. "It makes more sense that way. I wouldn't have thought of that, though. That means nobody's going to just ride out there and push them off. They've got some pretty high stakes in that little camp. Did anyone see you?"

"I don't think so. We didn't go back and look, though."

"I think we'd better call a meeting. This might change a lot of things."

"How long do you think they'll stay?"

"Just long enough to get the stuff out of here. They're probably handling more than that little bit you saw. But they won't need to stay there very long. As soon as they ship all they've got, that camp will be gone. You can count on it. They're just smart enough to use the agrarian front so no one gets suspicious."

"Do you think the other agrarians are in on this?"

Grandpa shook his head. "But right now we've got to worry about that bunch out on our place."

# Chapter Twenty

We were finishing supper when Uncle Travis came in. He pulled up a chair and put his elbows on the table with his hands in front of his face. "Before we meet with the others this evening," he began, "I figure we ought to have an understanding."

Grandpa pondered a moment and then pushed his plate back. He nodded his agreement.

"Where do we stand?" Uncle Travis asked.

"Has anything really changed?" Grandpa asked.

"You don't think so?"

"There's still a right and a wrong way to handle the problem. A wrong move at this point can ruin everything."

"There's already talk of getting rough with this third group."

Grandpa rubbed his eyes with the tips of his fingers. For a long time he didn't speak. When he did, he sounded tired. "Travis, we started on a course. It's the slow way, but I'm convinced that it will take us where we want to go. The other won't. I say we use the law."

"Using Carlos Alvarez can take a long time. You don't even have faith in Alvarez. We're not asking for much, just to keep what's legally ours. And if that means force, there are plenty that are willing to fight."

Grandpa stared at Uncle Travis. "Someone might get killed. Is it worth that?"

"Men have been defending their lands since the beginning of time. Men have been dying for their land for as long."

"How would you feel if we all charged out there and somebody from Juarez was killed?"

"I guess that's a chance we'd be taking. It's either fight or lose everything people down here have worked for for a hundred years."

"Is that little patch of ground west of San Diego worth somebody's life?"

"The land isn't the real issue."

"What is?" Grandpa asked.

"Our personal rights. Do we have a right to what is legally ours?"

"Seventy years ago we had a right to this land. But we left it. We chose the peaceful way. In retrospect, we chose the right way," Grandpa declared.

"If we ever leave the land again, there will be no coming back. We'll be finished in Mexico."

Uncle Travis looked down at the table. Grandma worked at the kitchen sink. She didn't comment or act as though she was hearing any of this. She continued washing dishes, but I knew that not a single word escaped her.

"Dad, some things are worth fighting for. Some things are worth dying for."

"But believe me, Travis, that little patch of dried-up dirt isn't one of them."

Grandpa smiled tiredly and breathed deeply. "After Harold and I were shot, there was a group of men that rode to my father's door. They had heard what had happened. They were coming to offer their support. And there was a bit of self-preservation there. If this thing could happen to Harold and me in broad daylight, what could happen to them and their own kids? They were ready to ride down there and clean the place out. I was barely conscious at the time. Even now I don't remember how much I dreamed and how much was real and how much has been told to me.

"I was literally hanging between life and death. Dad didn't know whether I would live. Harold was dead. His cattle had been stolen. There were those threatening to take his land. He had every right to ride down to San Diego and exact a little justice, a little vengeance. For a moment he held the whole town in his hands. At that moment he was the one man in the town who was able to say what would happen."

Grandpa shook his head. "There he stood on the front porch with the Juarez men in front of him. But he sent them home. You know, Travis, for the longest time I held that against my father. For as long as he lived, I felt he had loved me less for not riding down to San Diego and settling the score. I even thought him a coward." Grandpa stared across the table at Uncle Travis. "Now I stand on that porch. And everybody's going to judge me. That's a cruel twist of fate, isn't it, Travis? But you know, I understand now. I thought I had understood before. But I didn't. Travis, maybe you don't understand why I'm doing what I'm doing, but I'm asking you to stand by me until you do. Because I'm convinced that one day you will understand."

For the longest time Grandpa and Uncle Travis stared across the table at each other. Finally Uncle Travis pushed away from the table and stood up. "We'll do it your way," he whispered.

Grandpa pushed himself to his feet and started toward the door. "We might be a little late getting back, Martha," he said. He stopped and turned to face me. I was still at the table. "You coming?" he asked.

I hadn't even dared hope that I would be permitted to go. There had been other meetings, but I had never been extended an invitation. "Can I?" I asked hesitantly.

A smile brightened his face. "Don't forget, you're the man that called this meeting."

The men from Colonia Juarez were crowded into Calvin Cramer's huge living room. The windows and doors had been flung open to invite in the evening's coolness. Inside the room the air was warm and heavy. Grandpa, Uncle Travis, and I pushed our way into the room and found a spot next to José Luís, who had come at Grandpa's request. He was the only Mexican man in attendance.

In the beginning there was no real direction to the gathering, just a grumbling of complaints and unanswerable questions. Already, just hours after my discovery, everyone in Colonia Juarez seemed to know the third camp was dealing in drugs. Fear and speculation had fanned new rumors and created a cold tension.

It was obvious from the outset that there was genuine fear here. It was etched across the men's faces, implanted in their eyes, and carried in the tone of their voices. Over the years these men had learned to live with uncertainty and disaster. All were at the mercy of weather and capricious economic conditions. But through it all they clung to one constant — the land, their anchor in this sea of challenges and threats. Because of the land, they could combat the plunging peso, the sudden summer hailstorm that wiped out ten thousand trees of young fruit, or even workers' strikes that left ripe fruit rotting on burdened trees. But the agrarian problem threatened to cut the anchor chain. They were desperate for a solution.

"All right, men," Calvin's booming voice suddenly called out, bringing with it quiet and order to the babble of voices. "Let's get this thing organized." All eyes were on him. "We've been waiting for several weeks now, wondering what to do. I think it's pretty plain now." Calvin was in control. I thought it no accident that this meeting was in his home. I glanced at Grandpa. He sat quietly, staring down at his hands in his lap. He hadn't spoken to anyone. "We're not just dealing with a few poor folks looking for a little patch of ground to raise a garden on," Calvin went on. "We have men out there using our land to market their drugs. It's like someone has declared open season on our land. In the past we've had an occasional camp of agrarians move out on our land. But they've been downright timid compared to these last groups."

Ben Waltzer bounced to his feet. "If there's marijuana out there, we ought to ride out tonight and get it. There's enough of us. We could drive right down there, pick it up, and be gone before anyone knew a thing about it. We'd have the proof right in our hands. We could show the authorities why we wanted those people out of there."

"Exactly," Calvin declared. "Those drug runners thought they'd capitalize on the agrarian situation. Well, I think we can capitalize on the drug situation. That's our excuse to move now. And we better not let it slip through our fingers."

"But," Benjamin Wagner argued, "the other two camps aren't involved in drugs."

"That doesn't matter. They're out there illegally. This will give us a chance to get rid of the whole bunch of them."

There was a loud grumble of support.

"We've done a lot of talking during the last few weeks," Calvin Cramer cut in, taking control again. "There's been a lot of speculation as to what should be done. We really haven't been together. There are some of us who have wanted to move fast. There are others who have taken a more cautious approach." He glanced in Grandpa's direction, filled his lungs with air, and exhaled slowly. "I think the time for indecision is past. I say we need to move. Even tonight."

There was another grumble of approval.

"What do you think, Jake?" Reese Taylor spoke up.

Calvin glowered at Reese and then, like everyone else in the room, he turned to Grandpa. Even in his silence, Grandpa was the real leader here, and everyone in that room knew it. The others could rant and rave and present plans, but before the final decision was made, Grandpa would be heard.

Grandpa pondered momentarily. "There's an assumption here," he began slowly, "that this third camp makes everything easy. Because there are drugs in the camp, we just ride out and push them off the range. That camp gives us an excuse to clear the whole range." He shook his head. "If anything, the situation is more complicated now."

"You don't figure we should ride out and clean out this third camp?" Calvin questioned.

Grandpa shook his head. "First, we're not dealing with the same kind of people that are out on Shupe and Spilsbury land. They're not a bunch of farmers trying to scratch a living out of a patch of dry ground. They're sitting on a half ton of marijuana. And there's more where that came from. If that's a runway out there, the camp's temporary. It will only be there until they've shipped out their crop. Then they'll move on. Whether they come back later is yet to be seen. But those men are in the business of making money."

"That's why we can move them off," Calvin spoke out. "Once they know we know what they're up to, they're not going to hang around. And while we're at it, we hit the other two camps. That way we're just taking care of a bunch of thugs. Nobody's going to have any sympathy for a bunch of drug-dealing squatters."

"You're right there. But those men aren't a bit interested in public sympathy. I don't know what a half ton of marijuana is worth, but my guess is that it goes for a little more than apples and beef. That's big money out there. If it weren't, those men wouldn't be taking the risk. Those men are used to risks. They're used to fighting. Dirty. If we go charging out there, bent on taking their crop, they're going to put up a fight."

"Nobody's saying we should charge out there blindly. We don't even have to go to their camp. It's a quarter of a mile from where their camp is. We could load it up without them even knowing about it."

"Let's suppose, Calvin, that we go out there tonight and pick up that marijuana. What do we do with it?"

"Take it to Casas to the authorities. Let them know what's happening out here. Let them know why we want those people out of there."

"I wonder if there's anybody in Casas who knows what's going on out there on my range. I wonder if there's anybody in the police department who knows. I wonder how many men in Casas have a stake in that operation out there." Grandpa paused. "You can bet your last centavo that those half dozen men out there on my range aren't the ringleaders of this operation. The real operators are sitting back fat and safe. But they're going to look after their interests."

"Okay, there are people in Casas making money on this operation. I think we all know that. And there are authorities on the take. What's your point?"

"There are people in Casas with an investment in that operation out by San Diego. But we don't know who they are. So we're riding blind. We don't have time to find out who's on our side and who's not. We ride into Casas with a half ton of marijuana, and we might get picked up for drugs. We might end up in jail, the marijuana confiscated and maybe our land with it. And I'll bet that that marijuana would still make its way out of the country, and the finger of blame would be pointing squarely at the Mormons. Then we'd be the ones using our orchards and ranches as a front for our real crop— marijuana. Picking that marijuana up isn't our job. Not tonight it's not."

"So we just sit around?" Calvin argued. "And let them fly the stuff out? Maybe tonight."

"Maybe."

"Are you afraid?" Calvin demanded.

Travis was on his feet, his face dark. "Are you suggesting that Dad's afraid?"

"The thought crossed my mind."

Reese Taylor came to his feet. He pulled his pants up and tucked his shirt in. "There isn't anybody here that has as much right to ride in to those camps and clean them out as Jake does. It's not fear that's holding him back. Just brains. I'd like to hear someone say that he's a coward." He looked straight at Calvin. Calvin fidgeted and looked away. "I say we go with Jake's plan. There haven't been many times when he's taken us in the wrong direction. I've trusted him up till now."

"Would it be too much to ask what his plan is?" Calvin muttered.

"Carlos Alvarez isn't mixed up in this operation. He's had a reputation of being hard on the drug trade."

"And what makes you think he'd help us now when he hasn't so far?"

"Because this gives him the excuse to move. It might even give him a chance to strengthen his own position."

"By the time he moves, there won't even be a camp out there."

"I'll go to Chihuahua tonight. He'll talk to me. He might be here tomorrow."

"I'll go with you, Jake," Reese volunteered.

Grandpa smiled over at his friend. "I'd appreciate that, Reese."

"And what if they ship everything out tonight?" Calvin came back.

"They won't," Travis spoke up.

"And what makes you so sure?"

"Because we won't let them."

"How you going to stop them?"

Uncle Travis thought for a moment and then a smile spread across his face. "One of my boys was lost today."

"What?"

"I'm rounding up a search party to go look for my boy. I figure he might be lost out west of San Diego. We've got to find him tonight and we're going to be all over that country tonight with flashlights, camp fires, headlights. There will be so many of us out there that they won't dare bring a plane in or try to move that stuff out. We'll set up a main camp right down by the spring. We won't bother their marijuana cache, but we'll be thick as flies around there, so thick they won't even be able to think of moving that stuff."

Some of the men in the room began to smile and nod their heads.

"And if they get suspicious?" Calvin asked.

"They won't," Uncle Travis replied. "We'll go to them first thing, ask them if they've seen the boy. We'll let them know that we're going to be around looking."

"Are we going armed?" Calvin asked.

"Calvin," Uncle Travis pointed out, "we're looking for a lost boy, not hunting a mad dog. We don't need guns. Maybe one or two for a signal."

"And if Alvarez doesn't give us any help?" Calvin persisted.

"Then we'll try something else," Uncle Travis answered.

"Who's running the search party?" Calvin wanted to know.

"Since it's Travis's boy," Benjamin Wagner spoke out, "I think he ought to take the job. He's the logical choice."

# Chapter Twenty-One

Grandpa and Reese Taylor left that same night for Chihuahua City. The rest of us piled into trucks and began our
"search" for Uncle Travis's missing son. Every man and boy
above the age of sixteen was out west of San Diego and Cuautemoch, combing the country, flashing lights, calling out and
stomping through the brush and grass, doing everything we
could to make our presence innocent but obvious.

We hit the area so suddenly and with such force and enthusiasm that we took the squatters' camp completely by surprise. We were all over the country before they even had a
chance to ask questions.

We set up a camp by the spring where a huge fire burned
and plenty of food and drinks were available for the ones involved in the "search." It was arranged so that there was
continual traffic in and out of the camp. We wanted that area
thick with people.

The first thing I did when we arrived at the spring was to
check the cache of marijuana. It was still concealed in the brush
right where I had left it that afternoon. At least for this one
night, no one was going to move it.

"Do you think it's working?" I asked Uncle Travis a little
after 1:00 A.M. while we both huddled about the fire at the
spring.

"It's hard to tell, Jacob," he answered. "I rode into their

camp first thing. They seemed natural enough. Maybe they're not even connected with the stuff here. Maybe it's just coincidence." He laughed. "There's one thing for certain, though; nobody's going to get that stuff out tonight."

"Even if it's theirs, we can't prove anything, can we?"

Uncle Travis shook his head. "But Alvarez and his group might be able to prove something if they go into their camp."

"Can he just march into their camp without a warrant or anything?"

"If Alvarez really wants to know what's in that camp, the last thing he'll worry about is a warrant."

"Hey, Travis," Will Call rasped, bursting from the darkness into the yellow light of the fire. He was breathing hard and his face sparkled with beads of perspiration. "I was over on the promontory where Jacob figured the runway was." He wet his lips. "The brush is cleared off, stacked in little piles. It's a runway all right. All they've got to do is light those piles of grass and brush. They would burn for a few minutes — long enough to bring a plane down. A plane could swoop down, and no one would know the difference. It wouldn't be the smoothest landing, but it's good enough in a pinch. They're planning something and getting nervous. Paul Romney was over talking to them a while back. They're waiting for something. He's sure of it. They even suggested that we look someplace else for the kid, and they offered to check things out around here for us. They're nervous, Travis."

Uncle Travis nodded. "Several have been down here to the camp already. They're checking up on us, that's for sure. Looks like Jacob's hunch was right. The people in that camp know about this cache of marijuana."

"What do we do?"

"We hang tight. Now if Alvarez will only come through on his end."

The night dragged on and a cool edge developed in the black air. Whenever I wasn't around the fire, I wished that I had remembered a jacket or sweater, but I didn't let the night's coolness slow me down. Like the others, I tromped about the flats, flashing my light, calling out and making myself known.

It was almost three o'clock in the morning when we heard the buzz of the plane engine overhead. At first it sounded like the distant rumble of a truck coming down the road from the mountains, but as it approached, there was no question about it being a plane.

At the time I was with Uncle Travis, canvasing the brush. We both stopped and held our breath, our eyes following the blinking red lights of the plane flying overhead. The plane made a quick pass over the general area of the squatters' camp and then disappeared, only to reappear several minutes later, this time flying lower.

"That's them, isn't it?" I said.

"They're not sight-seeing, that's for sure," Uncle Travis muttered. "We need to call everyone into the camp. I want a big enough crowd down there that none of those squatters will be brave enough to try anything."

The plane flew over us, circling, searching, waiting for a signal from the ground. None came. In the meantime, Uncle Travis ordered three shots to be fired, the prearranged signal, and the searchers began moving back to the camp.

Four times the plane made a low pass overhead as though determined to land in spite of all the activity on the ground. Once the engine sputtered and died, but after a short moment it roared again and was off in the direction of Colonia Juarez. It didn't return.

"Do you think they signaled to them and sent them away?" I asked Uncle Travis.

"I doubt it. If they had had radio contact with them, they would have warned them off long before their first pass. And they would have never come back a second time. My guess is that the men in the camp were to have given a signal from the ground. They were probably expecting them to light the fires on the runway. All along they've figured they were completely safe out here. It was just a matter of dropping down, picking up the stuff, and flying out a few minutes later."

The rest of the night slipped away without incident. Soon dawn's golden fingers pierced the eastern sky and we knew our vigil was about over. A little after 5:00 A.M. I drove back to Colonia Juarez with Uncle Travis and Benjamin Wagner to pick up some food for the men that remained. As we were riding into town, Myrna Romney flagged us down.

"There's a plane out on the highway, between the dugway and the Tinaja," she called to us, leaning out her car window. Her eyes were wide, her face shadowed with worry.

"A plane?" Uncle Travis asked.

"It must have landed during the night. It's just sitting there off to the side of the highway."

"And the pilot?"

"Nobody's around."

"Do you think it was the one flying around last night?" I asked.

"It's got to be," Uncle Travis answered. "They were probably supposed to refuel out there at the squatters' camp. That's why they wouldn't give up. They weren't determined, just desperate."

"What do we do now?" I wondered.

"Somebody's got to stay by that plane," Uncle Travis said. "Nobody can pick it up. Whoever left it might be back."

"You don't think they'd just leave a plane there, do you?" I asked. "That's a lot of money."

"If they're hauling what we think they're hauling, the last thing that pilot wants is to get caught with that plane. My guess is that he is clear out of the country by now. He's just hired to fly the plane. Neither the plane nor the marijuana is his. He doesn't have to take the risk."

For the next four hours there was a tenseness in the air. Everyone waited. The pilot didn't return to the plane. There was no word from Grandpa. There was nothing, just a tedious wait.

Then shortly after nine o'clock the first troop truck rumbled into Colonia Juarez. Carlos Alvarez had flown to Casas early that morning and ordered the soldiers at the garrison in Casas along with several state policemen to drive out and investigate the squatters' camp.

Even with Alvarez moving as quickly and as secretly as he had, somehow the squatters on Grandpa's place were tipped off. When the troop truck arrived, the men were gone, leaving behind them their makeshift tents, a couple hundred gallons of fuel, and their cache of marijuana.

Alvarez took charge of the operation. He was a dignified, athletic man in his midforties, handsome and disciplined, a cross between an army officer and a bank executive. He ordered the marijuana doused with gasoline and burned. Directing the soldiers himself, he headed up the mountain road in pursuit of the squatters, leaving word that he would return as soon as possible to take care of the two agrarian camps on Shupe's and Spilsbury's places.

Grandpa called later in the morning from Chihuahua City and indicated that he would be late getting back to Colonia Juarez because he and Reese still had some business to take care of.

Around noon Alvin Shupe reported that the squatters' camp over on Spilsbury's place was breaking up and that the people were getting ready to move. They realized that it would only be a matter of time before the troops would be back from the mountains and that their camp would be next. The agrarians on Shupe's place were slower to respond, but even some of them began to pack their things and prepare to vacate their stolen section of range.

Colonia Juarez was in an uproar of excitement and speculation. It was difficult for anyone to grasp what had happened in just twenty-four hours. One thing was certain: Grandpa's way had proved slow in the beginning but quick and effective in the end.

The only person in the whole town who seemed the least

bit calm was Grandma. She went about her usual tasks, barely conscious of what was happening around her. Perhaps she had known all along that Grandpa would find the solution to the problem. She sent me into the garden to pick corn, squash, and green beans for Amanda Call, a widow in town. I was in the garden when a battered Ford truck rattled down the rough dusty road in front of Grandpa's place. The engine was hissing and steaming. The cab was packed with people, and the back of the truck was stacked high with the pitiful possessions of poverty. A heavy green tarp, which hours before had been the crude home of some of these people, covered the load. Several younger children and women and men with sad, staring faces rode on top. These were the first agrarians to move on.

At the corner where the road turned toward the bridge, the truck groaned, sputtered, and died. Slowly the people began to climb from the truck. Three men crawled from the cab and poked their heads under the hood.

I watched with interest from the seclusion of the corn patch. I couldn't help but wonder if Grandpa would like to view his triumph. He had been right. The agrarians had been forced to move. But as I watched, I knew Grandpa would feel no personal triumph. Only compassion. These people had threatened his land, his existence in Mexico, but as near as I could tell he had never resorted to hate.

I returned to my work, continuing down the row of corn, ripping off the plump ears. I piled the ears high in my arms and carried them to the front of the rows and stuffed them into a burlap sack. As I counted out the ears, I sensed someone watching me. I looked up to see three dirty little kids staring through the fence at me. There were two boys and a small girl, not much older than two or three. The boys were probably both under six. Their faces were dirty, their hair snarled and greasy. I had seen dirty kids before, but these were different. Their dirt was tattooed to their skin. Their eyes were dark and just a little sunken. They were eyes too old, too dejected, too defeated for children's eyes. If there was a light in life, these young eyes had never seen it.

Suddenly the little girl began to whine. *"Tengo sed."*

Understanding, I stepped to the hose, turned it on, and pulled it over the fence where each of the kids could get a drink. They drank until I was sure their bellies would burst. I enjoyed watching them, satisfied that I could help out. Then the thought occurred to me that only a few days before I had almost despised these people. I had wanted to ride out with Calvin Cramer and the others and crush them, drive them away. There were no thoughts of mercy then. Now I found that incredible. A foreboding kind of guilt nagged at my conscience.

The little girl, in trying to drink, squirted her older brother. He jumped back, surprised. Then the first traces of a smile emerged from his sober mask. He stomped his bare foot into the water and splashed his sister and brother. Soon the three of them were squirting each other, stomping in the water and laughing. I began to chuckle. Then, as suddenly as the jovial climate had emerged, it disappeared. Their young mother approached, looking first at me and then at the kids. She spoke in a harsh, rushed tone, and the children took a few backward steps and then turned and scampered toward the truck where the men were closing the open hood and preparing to move on. The young mother watched her children disappear, and then she looked down at the hose that was still running, its cool clear water spilling out onto the dry dirt. She touched her tongue to her lips and then started to turn.

*"Agua?"* I asked suddenly, grabbing up the hose and holding it out to her.

She hesitated, swallowed, and then nodded once. She approached suspiciously, reached out, and took the hose and began to drink. She wasn't much older than I. I imagined that she had been pretty once. Some of her beauty still clung to her, but it was rapidly vanishing under the relentless onslaught of premature age, worry, and discouragement.

When she was finished, she nodded thanks and turned back toward the truck.

Suddenly I was overwhelmed with an urge to help these people. The engine groaned and growled and the truck began to lunge forward. I became desperate. It was as though something were escaping forever from my life, and if I didn't grasp it I would regret it forever. I wanted to show these people — and myself — that I really didn't resent them, that I wasn't like Calvin Cramer and some of the others.

Without wanting or meaning to, I suddenly thought of the incident on the flats with Chet Cramer and Randy Hatch. I shuddered to think that I had actually stood by and permitted Chet's cruelty. In a desperate attempt to absolve me from that horror, I looked around for something I could do, something I could give. Anything! Then I spotted the burlap sack filled with Amanda Call's corn. It wasn't much, but it was something, and something tangible right now was better than all the best intentions five minutes from now. I could pick Amanda more corn, but if I didn't give these people something this instant, they would be gone.

It was strange that at that moment I thought of Arnold Gates. I pictured Grandpa as a young boy racing toward an old barn, bursting through the doors. And being too late!

I jerked up the sack and tossed it over the fence, leaped over the fence myself, and then sprinted after the departing truck. It was moving slowly enough that I knew I could catch it before it reached the bridge.

When I reached the rear of the truck, I swung the sack around my head once and tossed it up on the load next to the woman, who sat with her back to me.

Just then the truck gasped and jerked to a stop with the engine still running. The driver gunned the engine. The young mother looked down at me with uncertainty.

"*Es para usted*," I explained, panting and wiping my mouth with the back of my hand. "*Para usted y su familia.*"

Just then the woman's husband crawled from the front of

the load to where she sat. He looked down at me. Our eyes locked. I could feel my mouth dropping open and a tightening in the pit of my stomach. It was as though I were suddenly brought face to face with a horrible ghost. I saw the bruise about his left eye and the puffy but healing cut on his right cheekbone. He looked so different now from the day I had seen him on the flats. At that time I hadn't pictured him with a family. Or with anything else that would humanize him. He was just—just one of *them*. I had found it easy to condemn Chet Cramer for his prejudice and hate. Now I was sickened to realize that, in my silent hesitation, I had been as bad.

I swallowed in horror. The events of that late afternoon burst into my mind. I saw him suffering defiantly in the dirt, refusing to move the last rock from the road. I remembered his hateful but triumphant look as we drove past him, leaving him by the side of the road.

"*Es para usted,*" I mumbled. "*Y su familia.*"

I hoped that he wouldn't recognize me, but the darkening of the eyes, the tightening of the fists, the tension along his jaw all told me that he knew who I was. I was one of *them!*

The truck began to move. I stood frozen in the road as it moved away and swayed sluggishly toward the bridge. The man's eyes never tore away from mine. Slowly he leaned over, grabbed the sack of corn, and without ever looking inside, hurled the sack from him. It arched upward away from the truck and then plunged down into the quiet waters of the river. I heard the splash but never took my eyes from the man who stood beside his wife. I stood in the road watching until the truck turned at the corner and headed out of Colonia Juarez, gone forever. And suddenly I understood that not every Arnold Gates is abandoned in a barn.

As I stood there in the road, I thought of another agrarian. Perhaps he too rode in the same truck. I recalled his silent gratitude as Grandpa had defended him in front of Calvin Cramer and had sent him away with his portion of Grandpa's butchered steer.

# Chapter Twenty-Two

I was just crawling out of bed the next morning when I heard the truck pull into the driveway. I crept to the window and looked out. Gray shadows of dawn were still everywhere, but I noticed two things immediately. Uncle Travis had driven down the driveway, and Grandpa's car was still missing. When I had gone to bed, Grandma had still been waiting for Grandpa, wanting to have a warm meal on the table when he came in.

Uncle Travis stepped from the truck and headed for the kitchen door. I knew the door would be locked, so I decided to get up so Grandma wouldn't have to. If Grandpa wasn't home, she had probably stayed up past midnight and would be tired. I pulled on my pants and was stumbling down the hall to the kitchen when I heard Uncle Travis try the lock and then tap gently.

As I entered the kitchen and flipped on the light, I noticed Grandpa's place set at the end of the table, still untouched.

Tiredly rubbing my eyes and scratching my head, I un-locked the side door and threw it open. Uncle Travis stood there a moment and then stepped in without giving any kind of greeting.

"Where's Mom?" he asked bluntly before I could even close the door behind him. His face was troubled and pale. His jaw was clamped tight. The thought occurred to me that the pressures of the last two days were too much for him. He didn't have the hardened constitution that Grandpa did.

"I'll get her," I mumbled. "She's probably—"

"Travis," Grandma called quietly from the hallway. She had just come down the darkened hall in her robe and was standing in the doorway, sleepy and a little frightened by this early morning visit.

Travis looked at her a moment and then pulled out a chair and beckoned, "Come and sit down, Mom." He wet his lips and pointed to the chair. Grandma didn't move.

"It's Jake, isn't it?" she questioned, her voice shaking. Grandma shook her head without taking her eyes from Uncle Travis. Her lips were pressed together and she was gripping the front of her robe as though afraid to let go. "What has happened?"

Uncle Travis swallowed and brushed his hand in front of his face. "Dad's . . . " He leaned on the chair he had pulled out for Grandma. He swallowed once. "He's dead," he said in a hoarse whisper.

There was complete silence. For a moment no one moved. No one breathed. Grandpa dead? I squinted in disbelief at Uncle Travis, wondering if I was hearing all of this. I wanted to protest, but I had no voice, just a growing horror of what had just been announced. Never in my wildest fears had I suspected anything so devastating. And yet the sickened look on Uncle Travis's face left no room for hope.

Grandma stepped to the kitchen chair Uncle Travis held out for her. In her bare feet she made no noise crossing the kitchen floor. She sank into the chair and reached out to touch the table as though to steady herself. She was consumed by shock and horror.

Uncle Travis put a hand on her shoulder and squeezed. "They hit a horse," he began, his voice breaking, "about one o'clock this morning. Dad was driving, Reese was asleep in the back. They came around a curve. It was just there, in the middle of the road. You know how it is out there at night. There was no place to turn. It was either hit the horse or slam into the side of the mountain or go off the edge. It couldn't have happened at a worse spot."

Slowly Grandma pressed shaking hands to her mouth and wilted into a soft sob. Shaking her head, she whispered hoarsely, "No, no, no."

"Reese was cut and bruised a bit, but he's all right." Uncle Travis went on. "I spoke with him this morning. He wanted me to tell you. He said Dad didn't feel a thing. The horse came right through the windshield on top of him."

There was a long silence. None of us spoke. For several minutes we suffered in our own worlds, shedding silent tears while we groped for a reason for this stunning scenario.

It was all so unfair, such a cruel twist of fate. Grandpa had made it through life, overcoming numerous obstacles. More than once he had come face to face with death. He had lived with uncertainty, danger, and disaster. And in the end, he was killed on a dark road by a wandering horse.

"We'll need to call all the kids," Grandma said between sobs.

Uncle Travis nodded, "Carol was doing that when I left."

"I guess the funeral will have to be tomorrow. If we call now it should give everybody time."

"His body is in Casas. The Relief Society knows. They've already made arrangements to pick it up and bring it to Colonia Juarez. They'll have everything ready."

"Thank you, Travis." She reached up and touched his hand, which was still on her shoulder. "I appreciate you being here."

"You won't need to worry, Mom. I'll take care of every-thing."

"I know you will," she nodded, pressing her lips together again and swallowing. "Travis, right now—" Her voice began to break again as another wave of emotion washed over her. "Right now I'd like a few minutes alone."

Slowly she pushed herself to her feet and moved toward the place she had set at the table for Grandpa the evening before. She gathered up the silverware, set the glass on the plate, and carried everything to the cupboard.

"Travis," Grandma said, still holding the table setting, "your father did have one small request where his funeral was concerned."

"Dad talked about his funeral?" Uncle Travis asked, surprised.

"It was just something he mentioned." She shrugged, dazed. "A year or so back. He wanted his funeral in San Diego."

"In San Diego?" Uncle Travis gasped. He shook his head in disbelief. "Mom, you can't be serious! Not San Diego. That's so far out of the way. And there are going to be so many people. There's no room."

"He wanted it that way, Travis."

"I didn't ever hear him mention anything like that."

"He only mentioned it the one time. But Jacob was like that." She looked across the room, seeing nothing. "He loved San Diego."

"But, Mom, you can't be serious."

"We could have the viewing in the *casa de oración*."

"Mom, there's not enough room in that little house down there for the immediate family, let alone all the others."

"We can hold it outside."

"No one will be able to hear."

"Vernon Romney has those speakers. They would work. We could take chairs down. Travis," she choked, dabbing at her eyes, "your dad didn't ask for much. I would like to give him the little he did ask for."

Uncle Travis and I left Grandma alone. I went to my room, finished getting dressed, and went out to the barn. It had needed cleaning for some time. I had told Grandpa that I would do it, but I'd never gotten around to it. Now I attacked the task in a fury. I wanted to work. I had to work.

For three hours I labored like a fiend, mucking out the stalls, bringing in fresh straw, stacking boxes and buckets, sweeping and cleaning.

A little after nine o'clock people started dropping by. Uncle Travis returned for a moment to assure Grandma that the children had been called and all the other details had been taken care of.

When we left the house, he stopped by the barn. "I appreciate you helping out," he said as he stood in the doorway.

"I'll look after things on this end," I promised.

He nodded and looked away. He wiped at his eyes. "I wish I would have asked him more. There are a few things I would have wanted him to tell me."

"About the ranch and the orchards?"

He shook his head. "No, I know about them. There are other things, things more difficult to talk about. And even more difficult to understand."

For several minutes we stood there, both of us wrapped up in our own thoughts. "I called your mother this morning. She was leaving as soon as she could get away."

"Is she coming . . . alone?" I ventured.

"She didn't say. I didn't ask."

Just then Calvin Cramer drove into the yard in his truck. He pushed open his door, stepped out, and crunched across the gravel to where Uncle Travis and I stood. His hands were stuffed into his back pockets. He nodded a silent greeting, which Uncle Travis returned in kind. Then he leaned against the open barn door. "I'm sorry about Jake," he said quietly. "I only heard a few minutes ago. I was out working when Ben Waltzer stopped by and told me."

Uncle Travis nodded his acknowledgment.

"Jake and me didn't always see eye to eye, but there wasn't a better man in this valley. If there's anything I can do . . ."

"Thanks, Calvin."

Calvin took a couple of steps toward his truck and then stopped. "This agrarian trouble has cost us a good life, Travis."

"Calvin," Uncle Travis spoke, "it was an accident. There's no blame to be cast. He ran into a horse. No one's at fault."

"Travis, you know as well as I do that if he hadn't been

225

worried about those squatters, he would have never been in Chihuahua City. Those agrarians share part of the blame."

"Nothing's going to bring him back."

"No, but we can finish what he set out to do. There's still a pocket of them out on Shupe's place. They're dug in and plan to stay. Them hanging around like that is a mockery to Jake. You wouldn't have to go. There's plenty that would jump at the chance to help Jake this last time. Just give us the word."

Uncle Travis stepped away and looked about the place. It was his now. He could do anything he wanted. I remembered what he had wanted to do a few days earlier. Standing where he was standing right now he had told Grandpa that he favored throwing in with Calvin Cramer.

"Calvin," Uncle Travis began slowly, "Carlos Alvarez will be back today. He'll handle it."

Uncle Travis watched Calvin pull away. I came from the barn and stepped up behind him. Just then Guillermo Verdugo's oldest son walked into the yard and held out a thick envelope to Uncle Travis. "My father wanted me to bring this to you," he said in clear English. "It's the rent money. Jake wouldn't ever take it, but Papá thought you would need it now."

Uncle Travis looked at the envelope without taking it. He studied the Verdugo boy. "Guillermo's been saving the money?"

The boy nodded.

"Tell your dad . . . thank you. But tell him he should keep the money and use it to fix up the house. It's nice having you up by that north orchard. Your dad's looked after it real well."

The boy hesitated. "And next month?"

"I could use some help in the orchard. We could trade labor for rent. If it's all right with your dad."

"It's funny how much you learn about a person after they're gone," Uncle Travis reflected as he watched the Verdugo boy walk away. "I always knew Dad was generous, but I didn't know how generous until now. People have come to me— some people I hardly know—and told me things Dad did for them." He smiled wanly. "Can you imagine that? They come to me and thank me for what Dad did. Most of them were little things — a sack of apples, a few ears of corn, extra time with a water turn, a shoveled ditch, a fixed fence, a few pesos he didn't need." Uncle Travis shook his head. "He was a regular one-man charity organization. One old Mexican fellow told me that someone had left a box of groceries on his front step Christmas Eve. He didn't see Dad do it, but he thanked me just the same. I asked him how he could be so sure that Dad had been the giver. He shrugged and said that that was just something Dad would do."

The rest of the day I worked in the barn, the corrals, or in the hay yard. Late afternoon Reese Taylor came over with a load of hay. He was bruised and cut a bit about the face, but he looked in pretty good health.

"I wanted to leave everything square with Jake," he explained to me as he stepped from his truck. "I still owe him this load of hay." He ran his tongue over his lips. "I'm sorry about Jake. Real sorry. There wasn't a better man around."

Reese was still sore and weak and unable to really work, so I unloaded the hay for him. When I finished and was walking back to the house, I met Mom. She was alone.

# Chapter Twenty-Three

The next twenty-four hours passed as a blur. Family and friends descended, bringing with them words of condolence, mountains of food, and expressions of love and support.

I became lost in the crowds. I didn't even have a real chance to visit with Mom after our initial meeting in the yard. The morning of the funeral I left the house early, saddled one of the horses, and headed up the river. I didn't want to stay around the house and see the tears and hear the laments. I wanted to be off by myself—where Grandpa and I would have gone that day had things worked out differently.

As I rode up past the apple orchards, burdened with ripening fruit, and then along the river, I balked at accepting Grandpa's passing. I had never considered the possibility of Grandpa's death. Some people are never meant to die. They are just a part of life that is supposed to go on indefinitely. Life without them is strangely empty. How could that change so suddenly? How could a wandering horse on a country road destroy something so permanent?

All morning and into the early part of the afternoon I rode up the river, wallowing in my loneliness and sorrow. It was all so unfair. Grandpa was gone. With him went one of my life's last threads of stability. Just when my own family was crumbling and I needed him most, Grandpa was taken. Now there was nothing to fall back on.

In my silent wanderings I passed the fence Grandpa and I had built. It was just as we had left it that day, straight, strong, and secure, a piece of both of us. I rode past the branding corral and recalled the hours in the sun fighting bawling calves. I stopped by the river where Grandpa had told me of San Diego. Everywhere I turned I saw a bit of Grandpa.

I had been tempted to skip the funeral. After all, the man was gone. A person could pay tribute in other ways without going and staring at a closed box. But in the end I decided to go because I knew Grandma would want me there.

When I returned to the house, it was empty. Everyone had left for San Diego. Even the town itself was deserted. A quiet calm had descended as though in final tribute to the man who had done so much to build this town.

I hurried into the house, showered and put on my Sunday clothes, rushed out to the truck, and headed down the rough road to San Diego.

I was still almost a half mile from the town when I reached the first parked cars and trucks. There were people hurrying along the dusty road in the direction of the *casa de oración*. Mexicans and Anglos alike pushed on together to pay their last respects.

I'm not sure what I expected. I suppose in a way I had assumed that having the funeral in San Diego would mean a small crowd. A few of the faithful would make the trek. I had assumed that there, away from the mainstream of colony life, Grandpa's passing would go unnoticed. But as I approached the *casa de oración*, I saw literally hundreds of people — rich and poor, brown and white, young and old, member and non-member. Although the starting time of the funeral had come and passed, still the service was delayed as the people filed slowly through the *casa de oración* for one last glimpse at Grandpa.

I didn't go into the viewing. I chose instead to stay outside, lost in the crowd. I didn't want to see Grandpa in death. I wanted to remember him as he had lived.

There was a quiet reverence all about me. People spoke in hushed tones in both Spanish and English. Each person had come in his very best. Only a few had chairs to sit on. The others stood, but no one seemed to mind. All appeared glad to be there.

The funeral was to have started at two o'clock, but it was almost three before the casket was finally brought outside and the service itself began. Vernon Romney had set up a speaking system so that the people could hear, and there under the glaring sun the service proceeded.

There were several speakers, some in English, some in Spanish. I paid very little attention to what was said. My mind was elsewhere, trying to reconcile myself to Grandpa's death, trying to find some logic or justice to this turn of events. But in my pondering I found only frustration. It wasn't fair that the only human anchor I'd had throughout this uncertain summer had been snatched away. It was all I could do to stand there in the glaring sun and control the bitterness that festered inside me.

A flood of memories rushed upon me. I remembered Grandpa's quiet, powerful way, his penetrating blue eyes, his hoarse laugh, his gentleness. I recalled the day on the flats when he had ridden up to the agrarians. I had fought a lump of fear, but Grandpa had been cool and sure of himself. I remembered his sending me to the orchard to repair the damage of my neglect.

I remembered my first trip to San Diego, how he had driven down here, anxious with anticipation. A hundred other memories presented themselves, and then I began to catch a glimpse of understanding. People like Grandpa were immortal. The way they had lived made them so. Their influence was powerful and ever-present, whether they were hundreds of miles away, in the next room, or in the next life.

I looked up and saw the *casa de oración*, only a few steps from where Grandpa had sprawled critically wounded fifty years earlier. No one had cared then. But now the throng of people pressed forward to be with this gringo one final time.

And then I discovered what Grandpa had been trying to tell me all summer. I had assumed that Grandpa had showed me San Diego and told me his grisly tale so that I could understand him and this strange little village. But he had brought me to San Diego to understand myself. He had known all along what road I was destined to travel, because he had traveled the same road. We were to travel at different times and in different ways, but the road was the same. It had taken him years to make the journey. It had never been easy. But he had arrived. And when his life was over, he had San Diego to look back on. There was no reason for shame, no reason for excuses, no reason for regret. He had returned to San Diego and made it his, made it his as only he could.

Now the question challenged me: Did I have the courage to travel the same road? I hesitated. How could I? I clung desperately to a morbid dream of retaliation. I had a right to revenge. Would anyone deny me that after what Dad had done? The poignant storm raged within me. I didn't want to relinquish my hate. I didn't want to exhibit charity. I didn't want to turn the other cheek. I wanted to lash out. If even for a short time. Then there would be time for love and forgiveness—if that was my inclination. But right now I wanted the satisfaction of revenge.

But for Grandpa, I would have had my bitter portion of vengeance. As I stood in San Diego, I was a witness to his monument of love. My eyes filled with tears. My vision blurred. I blinked and the briny flood coursed down my cheeks. It had been years since I had cried, really cried; but that afternoon at Grandpa's funeral, I wept. And amidst my tears I wished more than anything that I could tell Grandpa that I finally understood.

When the benediction was finally pronounced and the people began moving toward their cars to return to Colonia

Juarez and the cemetery for burial, I turned and walked slowly to the truck.

"Jacob."

I turned. Laurie hurried up to me. She hesitated in front of me. "I wondered if you were here. I looked for you but—" She pressed her lips together. "Are you all right?"

I swallowed and nodded my head. "Yeah," I answered hoarsely. "I'm fine." I sucked in a breath of air.

"I'm sorry about Jake. I tried to see you a few times, but you were always gone."

For a moment we stood there, not knowing exactly what to say or do. "Do you want to ride with me?" I asked.

She smiled faintly and took my arm. We both walked to the truck.

I was glad she was there. Even though she said very little, it seemed that she understood how I was feeling.

"What happens now?" she asked as I started the engine and turned the truck around. "What are your plans?"

I cleared my throat. "I'm not sure how long Mom will stay. I'm sure she'll want to be with Grandma for a few days."

"And then what?"

"I guess she'll—we'll head back for Mesa."

"I suppose I knew, well, kind of figured that you would," she whispered. "Will you be back?"

I took her hand and squeezed. "I'll be back," I said. "What we've had here I want to last more than just a summer." I swallowed. "But there's something I need to do now. And I have to do it in Mesa."

"You plan to see your dad?"

I hesitated. I gripped the steering wheel. It was hard to verbalize what I had committed to do back in San Diego. Slowly I nodded. "Yes, I'll see Dad. I don't know what I'll say to him. I haven't planned that far ahead. But I will. I will. Things will never be the way I'd planned them, not where the family is concerned. But I can't change that. I guess the only thing I can do is to change how I feel about everything." I took a deep breath. "A few hours ago I wondered what possible good could come from Grandpa's death. I struggled with that. I don't know all the answers, but I can see more clearly the answers to some of my own questions."

"I'm glad you're going to see your dad."

"For a long time I've wondered if I could. After today, I know I can."

"I'll miss you, Jacob."

I smiled. "Just don't pick up strangers while I'm gone and take them to Casas for pizza."

"Not a chance."

"Good," I smiled, "because I'll be back. Soon. There are still some things I have to do in Colonia Juarez."

"It will be different with Jake gone," she whispered.

I didn't answer, because he wasn't gone. He would never leave Colonia Juarez. And more than ever, he was with me; and that made returning to Mesa and facing Dad seem possible. Grandpa had traveled the road to San Diego. Though reluctant, I was confident that I could now travel the road to Mesa.